Cyprus

A TASTE OF YESTERDAY

By

ELENI PROTOPAPA

D1729271

ΚΥΠΡΟΣ CYPRUS

1) Argaki
2) Katokopia
3) Morphou

4) Zodia
5) Nicosia

131 Coral Bay Avenue
Paphos 8575
Cyprus

Tel. 26-623364

NIKIANNA PRESS.

ALL RIGHTS RESERVED

No part of this publication may be reproduced, stored in a retrievable system, or transmitted in any form, or by any means without the permission in writing of the Author.

ISBN 9963 - 9316 - 0 - X

Dedicated to my grandchildren.

George, Eleni-Athena, Nikianna, Stella, Nicholas, Nikolas,
Philip, Sofia and Eleni-Teresa
As a record of our past less it be lost for ever
And to my husband for his help and support.

I would like to thank the Pafos Writers'Group for
listening to my stories, the first chairwoman of the group
Susan Down, the present chairman Bryan Drake and specially my
son-in-law Professor Elias Dinenis.

The door to our house
Big, wide, tall and solid, so wide to allow the oxen to go through yoked

In memory of my parents
and the people of Arghaki
who died in exile

TABLE OF CONTENTS

8

LIST OF RECIPES

CHAPTER 1 - MY BIRTH PLACE

I was born in the mixed Greek and Turkish village of Arghaki. I grew up in two old and beautiful houses. One belonged to my grandparents and the other to my parents. My cousins who inherited my grandparents' house demolished it and they had an ugly coffee shop built and some even uglier shops. As far as I know our house is still standing. My parents' house would be protected if the Turkish Army did not now occupy the village. These houses like some people, both Greek and Turk, reflect what I am. We lived in these simple houses, authentic, traditional, functional and full of light, serving the

A pair of oxen yoked together

needs of the people and the animals alike. In the days I was growing up animals were almost as important as people.

I remember the people and their struggle to make a living. Everybody had to struggle, rich and poor alike. But the struggle was harder for the poor. These people still live vividly in my mind. I think of one of my grandfather's brothers, Pelavas, who had seven sons. He and his wife Preza worked very hard just to provide some food for them. They grew up to be good solid men and their children are very successful, with good jobs and houses of their own.

Arghaki was a mixed village for as long as people can remember. It was a happy village; people worked very hard at all times of the day and during the night watering the orchards. Men used to eat their kleftico (lamb baked in a clay oven) and drink their brandy in the coffee shop grouped round the tables, usually making sure that some kleftico was sent home to the wife and the children.

The Turks were a part of this picture. They lived all over the village and felt they belonged. They were on good terms with their neighbours and quite often they worked for each other. Their relationship was friendly even at the worst times of tension created by politics. In December 1963 many of the Turks in the island moved to the North part of Cyprus, obeying the orders of the Turkish leaders. But our Turks remained in the village where they felt they belonged, and where they felt safe.

The Denktash regime was not happy, as Arghaki was there to prove that Turks and Greeks could and would live together happily. So they sent five buses to take all of them to Lefka, one of their ghettos. Two prominent villagers, (one was my husband, and the other was one of my cousins) assured them that they would be safe and they could live in harmony like they had for years. The grown ups went into a Greek coffee shop where they had a lengthy meeting. They came out and they sent the five buses away. As a result no teacher was sent to teach the eight young Turkish children. A young graduate of the Turkish Lyceum was employed and paid by the parents to teach the children.

Very often I think of Ahmet the kind Turkish Muktar. His wife Sitika and their two sons lived in our neighbourhood. They were loved and respected by all of us. My father's cousin Rodou (Rose) who lived near our house was always there in the afternoons to help me take the huge saucepan with the black eyed beans off the wood fire and change the water according to my mother's instructions. The food had to be ready for the people who worked in the fields.

My grandmother had a Turkish friend called Hapipe. She was a tall slim woman who always dressed in white, in something that resembled a boorka. She was a formidable woman; children were scared of her and so were many women. She and my grandmother were quite good friends in a strange way. They helped each other in many ways. Hapipe Hanoum taught my grandmother to make good halloumi.Her husband Salih was a good shepherd with many sheep. My grandmother offered her flour and anything else she produced. I still remember how my grandmother would take all the food that was left over on the last day before fasting began, to Hapipe Hanoum. She would accept it, not as charity, but in the spirit in which it was given. Food was a gift from God so it was respected. It had to be. We as children tried to have glimpses in her house as we imagined that many strange things happened in her yard. Her daughters had painted nails, something unusual to us.

I had another Turkish friend of my own age. She was called Fatma; she lived in the centre of the village near the coffee shops. She knew Greek and we played together often.

Next to our house lived Kyria Morfini with the seven children. Her daughter and her two elder sons were my closest friends during

13

the tender years of my childhood. We shared many things; we even had the same surname, as our fathers were cousins.

I never realised, until recently when I started to write about my village how many people helped me become what I am. Now when I start to think about my village so many people come into my mind. Sometimes I feel I must write about all these people. They belong to a world lost to me; but they are my people.

My home is near Morphou. The Turkish Army has occupied Arghaki for many years, like so many towns and villages in the northern part of Cyprus. Although the house and village is occupied by people who do not cherish it the way we did, we still love it and consider it as our home and we believe it is there waiting for us.

When I was a young girl, opposite our house, there was a stream, which in winter had water most days; later with the building of dams it very seldom carried water. Just beyond the stream there were many threshing fields. These fields were our playgrounds. The children of our neighbourhood played there until the sunset. Quite often I played with the boys, I played their games. Those were happy years; I had a sense of belonging. Each day would be followed by one exactly the same.

When I close my eyes I find myself wandering round the house, in all the different corners. In the stable with the beautiful oxen, the mules, the silver coloured donkeys. These memories bring me back to my younger years when I tried, during school holidays, to help in feeding the animals, to draw water from the well to satisfy the thirst of people and animals.

In my memory, I recall the huge mantra, a huge enclave without a ceiling where large numbers of chicken, ducks, geese, and guinea fowls were kept. There was always a pig, which was destined to contribute to the diet of the family and the farm workers. Every afternoon the door of the mantra would be opened and all the birds, excited, fluttering and cackling would rush out into the big yard to enjoy the freedom offered. My mother scattered wheat around, while imitating their cackle so as to gather them around her.

Quite late in the afternoon, as the sun was setting, the ploughman would enter our big door with two handsome oxen yoked together - to me the most handsome in the village - and he would lead the oxen to the tub, which had been filled with cool water drawn fresh from the well. When the ploughman led the oxen into the yard my mother would stop whatever she was doing to help him take off the yoke and lead them to the stables. Their mangers had been filled with straw and hand ground Rovi (vicia ervilia) or Vicos (vicia sativa,) which was often mixed with hand broken broad beans. The ploughman had his share of attention; he would be offered a cup of coffee with a glass of cool water. Quite often some seasonal glyco (candied fruit in syrup) would accompany it. He would then go home to wash and change; later in the evening he would come back to a substantial supper and plenty of wine from a mountain village – we did not make wine on the plain.

I remember so clearly the stores for the straw; two huge rooms with sky windows. (Skylights). These were filled with straw when the threshing of the wheat and barley was completed. The straw was almost as precious as the wheat as it was needed for feeding the animals. What really impresses me, even now, is the way these stores were filled. Apparently the straw could not be carried to the store through the door; it had to be thrown through the sky window as this was the safest way. In the village there were certain men I remember like Kougioulis, who specialised in this job. Woven sacks were filled with straw and carried on donkeys by boys to the ladder, which led to the roof. Specialised workers, like Kougioulis, carried these sacks on their shoulders and climbed the wooden ladder up to the roof - these houses were very high. They then untied the sack and they emptied the straw through the sky window into the straw store.

By the time he came down the ladder, another sack was brought on the donkey ready to be carried to the roof. This was always done at night and stopped before the sun rose.

Needless to say, these people were given good wages and very good meals at a time when food was not so plentiful. My father, and later my husband never had any problem in finding the right people, as my mother provided the best meals in the village. In winter, the sky windows were closed and sealed with mud made from alluvial soil to keep out the rain.

Next to the straw stores stood the stable, a long room with plenty of mangers. There was space for the beautiful oxen, the mules, the donkeys and their little ones. Most of the donkeys I remember were silver coloured. The animals were indispensable for the work on the farm. They were also a source of pride. When they became sick, they were a focus of pain and worry, as there were no veterinary doctors readily available. Farmers had to rely on the wisdom of some villagers. As a child I remember a beautiful cow dying, and the grief of my parents and grandparent who was always advising and helping us in everything concerning the work on the land. Some time later a silver coloured donkey died while giving birth. It was very sad. They also had the task of moving the corpses and finding a place to bury them.

I shall try to write something about the house, although it is not very easy for sentimental reasons. The house is old and built of mud bricks. The people who needed them made mud bricks in the village with the assistance of their relations. When my parents became betrothed, or rather during the negotiations, my grandmother insisted that her daughter lived in the house without her in-law relations. As my father was determined to marry my mother, my paternal grandparents promised to give them the house. In those days the marital home had to be provided by the husband. It was very difficult for my grandparents to part with the house and move to another not so grand and spacious on the other side of the village. They had

16

another five children; the youngest was one year old. They moved to a house that had belonged to my father's maternal grandfather. There was a lot of land around the house where more houses for children and grandchildren could later be built. From what information I can collect, our house belonged to Haji Zenios Raftis. The word Raftis means tailor. As the head of the family was known as Raftis, tailor, all this family in the village is known as Raftides. In those days a tailor made what men wore, zimbounia, a colourful top made of hand woven material and sayies a longer garment. Haji Zenios was the son of Papaloizos who died in 1887 and whose father came from Paliometocho. I am sure that Haji Zenios Raftis lived in that house; he was my father's grandfather. Most probably his great-grandfather had lived there before him.

The house needed a lot of work. They had to build the outside wall to protect the yard and to build another wall to separate their mantra, from the mantras of the neighbours, who were all related to us. They had to finish the outside wall and enclose the big yard. My grandfather Anastasis, my mother's father, was a proud hardworking man; he wanted to make the house as presentable as possible. So they set out to make mud bricks and start to build the walls and protect the house. My parents worked very hard although they were young. My mother must have been around fifteen years old.

Mud bricks were not made on a commercial basis, but were made by the individuals as and when they were needed, with some assistance from relations, friends or a builder. They were made with red soil, which they brought from the fields and straw to hold the mud together. A lot of water was needed to mix the soil and the straw and make it into mud. In my parents' case the water had to be drawn from the well of the house. Mainly my mother undertook this job, while my father mixed the mud with a spade. He used to shovel the mud into a wooden box (tsivera), which had two long handles on each side to enable two people to carry it. My father with the help of another man

17

carried the mud and one of them, or if necessary, my mother, poured it into moulds, which were made by simply nailing pieces of wood together. Usually two moulds were joined together. In those days mud bricks were about 18 inches square and one and a half inches thick. The walls of our house are more than that because of the plastering. Mud bricks and the thick walls are very good insulators. Our house was cool in the summer and warm in winter. In later years, the villagers made them smaller in size. The first job was to build the outside wall and protect the yard. Then they built the mantra wall to create some privacy. The next jobs were more difficult as they needed more planning and specialised people.

The roof of my house, like other similar houses, is nearly flat, with slight inclinations on either side. In the villages of the Morphou area all houses of that period had flat roofs, which were used like a yard. When flax was brought in after it had been soaking for several days in a special ditch with the stagnant water, it was then taken onto the roof and left there to dry. Black-eyed beans were spread out to dry; there were many other farm products. The roof provided not only plenty of space for the different crops, but at the same time it protected them from the animals that might escape at any time from their shed.

The main house was very high and we had a big sturdy ladder made of wood. Round the yard were more rooms like the room with the well. These rooms were not so high and I found it easier to climb up there. In the summer we would often take a mattress on the roof and sleep there while my father went on night watch to sleep at the watermelon field. These houses were next to each other, sometimes touching together. The owners of these houses, like many other families, would put their mattresses out on the roof. There was a lovely feeling of belonging. We all slept under the stars. The only disadvantage was that we woke up very early before the sunrise.

The making of the ceiling and the roof was a work of art and ingenuity. They first placed the beams, which were well finished and varnished so they would last for many years. Across the beams they placed canes next to each other and tied tightly together. Some houses did not use the canes next to each other. Some, like ours, used crushed canes and had them woven in beautiful patterns. This is called a psatharka. On top of the canes or the psatharka they placed special wild shrubs which grew in places with stagnant water. I suppose that in other areas they used another type of shrub.

On top of the shrubs they threw a lot of alluvial soil. This is of a much lighter colour than ordinary soil. In the village they called it white soil. It was found on a piece of land next to the river so it was also called the village's soil. Anybody and everybody from the village were entitled to get as much soil as they needed. In winter, when the river flowed in spate, the soil was replaced. This special alluvial soil is less porous than any other soil and so it does not allow the rainwater to get through. Afterwards they used a trowel to spread the mud, which they made by mixing this special soil with water and straw.

The straw is a binding medium in the process. New thin layers were added almost every year. On top of this they used to add, especially on the sloping parts, a much stronger alluvial soil, known as 'konnos' in Greek. At different places along the roof edges, pieces of bent tin were placed to make short, gutter-like outlets. The edges of the roof were shaped to lead the water to the nearest metal outlet. These outlets did not lead to the ground; they extended about one foot from the edge. When it was raining they looked like small waterfalls. We as children quite often went under these waterfalls to have fun to the anger of our parents.

One big job was to have the whole house plastered. The rooms were not many but they occupied a lot of space. To enter the house there was a big, wide and tall solid door. It was so wide to allow the oxen to go through yoked. The door led to the long iliacos (used like a veranda, but it was not raised off the ground.) The floor of the iliacos was finished with fitted stones, small and beautiful. About one

19

yard after you enter there was a very low step. The iliacos was long with three decorative arches made of the yellow Yerolakkos stone. Just inside the house in the iliacos on the left there was a small long room, which had two windows. In the room right at the far end there was a beautiful Victorian bed draped with silk, hand woven by my mother. There was a big cupboard made of solid walnut; it was full of hand-woven materials. There was another beautiful piece of furniture, again of solid walnut, which was not very functional, displaying a number of nice things like old lamps and beautiful glassware. In the corner opposite the window there was a fine sofa of the kind you see in antique shops.

Right above the sofa, on the wall, there was a rectangular picture beautifully embroidered by my mother, with flowers and the phrase in calligraphic letters in Greek - 'Destiny cannot be avoided'. As a child I spent many hours trying to read it and many more to understand it. There was another picture of a bird with flowers. They would be considered naïve art today.

There were many family photographs of grandparents, uncles and aunts. At the other end of the room, there was a longish table with two drawers, placed against the wall; this table did not have the same character as the other pieces of furniture. It was a later acquisition when my father became involved in many village committees and the president of the village. It was used as a desk.

Next to this room was the most beautiful and functional room in the house. This is the dichoro, which means 'two spaces,' but it could easily make four rooms. The room in the middle has an imposing arch and it leads to another small room, known as the 'inner room' of the house. Incidentally in this room the actress Eleanor Bron spent a week.

When I was a child this room was used as a store. In the corner there was a big pithari, storage pot, where flour was placed after it was brought from the mill and spread for a few hours to cool down. There were big jars with halloumi cheese, big bottles full of olive oil, in straw baskets. Several medium size pitharia (earthen jugs), tarred inside with a special tar, were filled with black and green olives. The big Lapithos pots, glazed inside, were full of homemade sausages and lountza lightly fried and kept in lard. Everything had to be planned for feeding the farm workers. Together with all this food there were two or three special baskets filled with nicely folded clothes.

When my father died suddenly aged only fifty-five, my husband Nicos took over the farm and the problems that go with it. We used this room as a bedroom. Behind the dichoro were the several straw barns. Nicos loved this house as he had grown up in a similar one now owned by his brother, but at the same time he wanted our comfort. So he opened a doorway to one of the stores and he had a kitchen built and a shower next to it. The kitchen kept to the style of the house.

In the dichoro we had four beds, one in each corner, and the room was still not full. It is worth mentioning that these beds were on wheels and our children would draw them out in the summer and sleep in the iliakos or even in the yard under the sky. Just before the sun rose we would draw the beds inside so they would get some sleep whilst we would get on with whatever we had to do. Besides the beds there was a square table in the middle of the room, and against the wall a cupboard for hanging clothes and another with glass doors where one could see the most beautiful pottery and glassware. They would be considered collectable antiques these days.

The most interesting feature of the room was the plastered, decorated shelf attached to the wall, all around the room. On this shelf stood the best old plates I have ever seen and several elegant pots, 'merreches', for sprinkling rose water or blossom water on the hands of visitors or in church on special days. In later years, three chests were added to the room. Nicos had bought the first one from some people who were demolishing their house so they were pleased to sell. It was characteristic of the Lapithos way of carving with beautiful motifs without any colour. The other one was higher with bold coloured motifs. This was the traditional Akanthou type. They were both full of beautiful hand-woven materials. The third one was even bigger as people who had no space to store it gave it to us. This one was plain but solid; in it we kept our huge tent. Yet still the room did not feel crowded.

On one side on the wall there was the door, which led to the loft. There was not a permanent ladder to access the loft - every time we needed to climb to the loft, where my father kept the wheat and the barley we had to fetch a wooden ladder. In later years Nicos stored old farming tools in the loft, hoping to start a museum.

Next to the dichoro there was another room, which was used for many purposes. It had a low ceiling compared to other rooms, which all had very high ceilings. The loft was on top of the third room. Outside this room Nicos built a wooden balcony with a wooden staircase. The children loved to play up there. Here I must mention that the iliacos was the perfect place to eat breakfast and dinner. We had a big bench table. It was quite a long way from the kitchen but we had a trolley on wheels, which proved a great help.

When you lived in these houses, you realised the wisdom that went in planning and building them. Our house was very cool as it was built of mud bricks of a very good size. At the far end of the iliacos there was a high window, which brought a nice breeze. One day when we had a builder for other jobs, we asked him to close the little window. The iliacos was not the same. A little thing like a high window made all the difference.

Beyond there were the stables with a door that led to the first straw store and beyond that there were another two huge stores one of which Nicos turned into the kitchen. Outside the stable at the far end of the yard you could see the door to the mantra where the animals were kept. The room with the well was opposite the stable. We used to call this room 'the well'. Outside this room there was a natural stone sink where the animals quenched their thirst. In the room itself, there was the well and another stone sink for washing. At the other end of the room there were two fireplaces where we cooked over a wood fire big quantities of food in big copper saucepans. These fireplaces were on a bench made with stones and mud. Lower down there was another fireplace for a huge copper pan with two handles, as two people were needed to put it up or bring it down. In this pan they made the halloumi cheese, prepared the pourgouri, or made trahanas.and many more things.

When the house was renovated all this was taken down. Until the death of my father the back part of the yard was planted with trees and flowers. When Nicos took over the work of the farm we bought a lot of mechanical equipment, which had to be stored in the yard. The trees were felled and a special gate was installed. In the yard, not far from the gate, there were three ovens: one for bread, one for a roast or a mousakka, and a small one for kleftico. It was a small simple house with many possibilities and a lot of atmosphere. I very much hope we see it again before we die.

Scythes for harvesting

CHAPTER 2 - MY GRANDMOTHER

My grandmother was called Eleni. She was married to Anastasis Loi, and so she was known in the village as Anastasena. Anastasis, my grandfather, was a hardworking man. He had a wider knowledge of the world than any other man did in the village as he had worked for a monk in Avlona and Archangelos monasteries, which were part of Kykko Monastery. Anastasis was a good husband, and later a good father. They were a devoted solid couple.

Her mother was Anna, known as Hadji Anneza as she had visited the Holy Land in those days when very few people travelled. She had four daughters, who were known as Hadji Annezes in the village. They were considered to be very clever in everything that was held important in those times: cooking, sewing, weaving, keeping a good home, being careful with food and money, and, of course, being very clean.

My grandmother was fair, with green eyes, not very tall, but slim. It is unfortunate that my mother did not take after her. It is said that she has taken after her paternal grandmother: a little dark, on the plump side, with an "interesting" face. My great aunt, my grandmother's sister Kyriakou, was known in the village as Halloumena because her husband was called Halloumas. She was also very fair, but the third sister, Sofia, known as Dimarchena, was quite dark. The youngest daughter, who died when I was about a year old, must have been quite fair judging by what her children look like. These Hadji Annezes women were known in the village for the good management of their homes. Those who did not like them accused them of stinginess, but all those who had the chance to know them or to work with them spoke of their wisdom, both in running their homes and in managing the land and its produce.

My grandmother wore dresses with long skirts and well fitting tops. These she sewed for herself, by hand, with such fine stitches that you wouldn't believe it was hand-worked. Not only did she make all her own dresses, she also wove most, if not all, the material for her own clothes and for her husband's: the vrakes, [breeches] his shirts, and the tops known as zimbouni. I believe she was among the best weavers in the village, as she was not only clever, but extremely patient too. On account of this my grandfather was quite often exasperated with her, although he would agree that everything she set out to do would turn out almost perfect.

Hand weaving requires tremendous patience. First, the cottons had to be bought; when she ordered them, she would order the best dyes and dye the cottons herself. Red was used a lot, but black and green were also used. She would also use some of the threads she produced herself from flax or silkworm. When they wove mattress covers, they always used red cottons or red dyes, both in the warp and in the weft. Though I still have some of this material in my cupboard, I have not used it, as I feel it would be wasted on a mattress cover.

The threads in the warp had to be starched to make them stronger. For this, she would make gruel in a saucepan over the wood fire. First she would boil water, and then she would throw in a marble – sized piece of beeswax to help prevent the threads from tangling. Next she would start sprinkling in flour until it began to swell and the gruel thickened. The mixture was then removed from the fire and left to cool. More water was added until the gruel was of a thin coating consistency. Then the cottons were put into the mix and pressed down well to make sure they absorbed it properly. They were then taken out, shaken, and passed over the special cane bobbin.

As children, we looked forward to the day when my grandmother made gruel, as we were given some with carob syrup or sugar, before

A woman spinning

it was diluted. Whatever it was served with, it was most welcome, because in those days cakes and cookies were not part of our diet. Friends and neighbours would drop in for some gruel with their children.

My grandmother discovered another way to starch the cottons. She made dough, shaped into pittes about a centimetre thick, which she cooked lightly on the wood fire, using something that resembled a Chinese wok, but more curved. She then crumbled the pittes, made them into dough and then into gruel. By doing this, she cooked the flour twice and she found this had better results.

From what I can remember, and from talking to my mother, who was born in 1908 preparing the weft was a very time-consuming business. After the cottons had been starched, they were wound on the specially prepared big cane bobbins. Grandmother's entrance hall was eleven picks long: a pick is sixty centimetres, and was until recently the standard measure before the metric system was introduced. My grandfather had to organise the hall according to my grandmother's instructions, so that she would be able to put the warp together. This meant a lot of work, as she often used at least two colours, and she had to estimate how much cloth she would get out of so much cotton; as she used different kinds of cotton for each sort of weaving. I can remember her clearly in that entrance of hall, counting

Weaving at the loom

the threads and talking it over with my mother who was a competent weaver herself.

It is important to remember that weaving in those days was as indispensable as farming and growing your food. Housewives had to be mistress of many crafts simply in order to survive, help her husband and bring up the family. My grandmother was an expert in all the crafts needed, both in the house and on the land.

My grandfather, too, was as good in his own way, and they made a very efficient team. Because of this, they acquired more land and became very successful in farming. They built a good name in the village. Grandfather was either president or committee member in several village concerns, such as the church and the irrigation committees. Grandmother kept very good accounts, as well as her household and farming duties. On Sunday, they would load the donkeys or mules with whatever they had to sell, and take it to the market in the town of Morphou. They sold their produce and then purchased whatever they needed for the week. She would not only buy the right things, but she would keep and use them very wisely.

If a villager were looking for something, they would always go to my grandmother. If she didn't happen to have it, no one else in the village would be expected to have it either. She would go to the religious fairs, usually with my grandfather; sometimes he would buy or sell an animal, donkey, young mule or a calf. Here she would buy whatever she needed for the house from the people who came from the mountain villages. They sold things like nuts, raisins, soutjoukko [a grape-juice and nut confection] and fruit. Often she would take her own farm produce to sell; pourgouri, homemade noodles or even flour were exchanged for products from the mountains. Nowadays it is difficult to imagine that time when there were no shops to buy things from, few people were in a position to travel, and those that did went by donkey or mule. So, if something was bought from a fair, it was made to last.

Good housekeeping took many forms: my mother tells me that grandmother would buy winter pears and hang them from the ceiling of the storeroom to ripen. If she went to visit someone who was sick, she would take a couple as a gift.

Every day, she would sweep the big room where we all assembled each evening for supper. This was a large gathering, which included my parents, the man who worked for us on a permanent basis, often

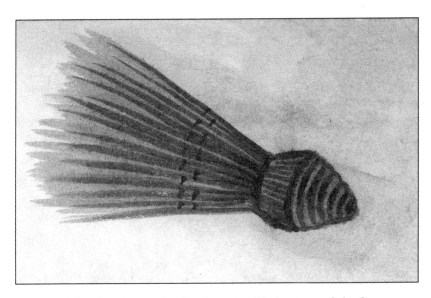

A handmade sweeping brush made with dry stems of shrubs

my aunt, uncle and several children. She would then sweep the two halls, known as 'iliakos' in Cyprus; the big yard, then the stables and finish by sweeping the road outside the house.

When the house adjacent to theirs was to be sold, which was very unusual in those days, my grandfather bought it because he did not trust or like the people who were interested in buying it. According to my mother he said to my grandmother, "If they come, we leave", so he had no alternative. He was a very determined person. By buying the new place and joining it with theirs, they had a double house in one. This is the house I knew where both my cousins and I had a lot of fun playing, watching everything and mainly growing up happily.

Now they could really expand. They had two dichora; the second one had a big fireplace and several inner rooms for storing straw and other farm produce. What I remember vividly is the corner in the straw store where a hen could often be seen sitting on the eggs to hatch them. My grandmother would look after her two or three times a day, making sure that she had enough food and water so that she did not desert her eggs. We were not allowed to visit the hen but secretly we always had a peep. Perhaps this is how we got our first unconscious knowledge of the role of the cock, as my grandmother was so specific in her selection of eggs; she made sure that she got the eggs for hatching from a chicken coop where there was a strong active cock. With the acquisition of the other house, there were more stables, a bigger yard and an open enclave for chicken and a pig. At

Cooking bread in the wood oven

the end of the yard there was an oven. My grandmother baked bread every week. She sieved the wheat flour very well to get rid of all the bran, she mixed the bran with barley flour to make small loaves for the dogs. Sometimes she double baked those. The baking day was a feast day. She would make olive bread, pumpkin pies; halloumopittes

31

[pies with halloumi] and she put a few potatoes and some eggs in the ashes to make a nice salad for the evening meal.

She always made a point of giving a piece of warm bread to a neighbour or a passer-by. If she did not find anybody to offer some warm bread to, she would leave a piece on the roof of the oven. She was very careful but at the same time very generous. Her brother in law had seven sons who spent much of their childhood in my grandmother's house. They had food there very often, when food was not plentiful but they helped whenever they could; they still have respect for my mother.

Her sister Sofia and her children spent a lot of time there and very often shared the good things that my grandparents would offer; one of her sons spent some years staying with my grandparents and working for them. He never showed the same respect. There was a nephew of my grandfather who took advantage of her decency and her generosity; He not only kept his sheep in my grandparents' big yard, he used their straw and barley and neither he nor his sister ever bothered to sweep the yard.

I mentioned some examples of her decency and generosity; I would also like to mention how careful she was to avoid unnecessary expenses: when she was not weaving or doing a job that needed light, she would lower the lamp to save the paraffin. When her sister Sofia asked why, she would say, "It is enough we do not work, we do not need to waste paraffin too."

Before the Second World War there were no cars in the village. In 1942, when I went to school in Nicosia, there was only one car in Katokopia. This was the vehicle that brought us to the village every Christmas and Easter Holidays and took us back to school. There was the train, which ran from Famagusta to Nicosia to Morphou to Xeros where the mines were. In those days the villagers along the railway line used the train to go to Nicosia. The first couple of years, after the holidays my father or my grandfather took me to Nicosia, to school, by train. The railway station was outside Nicosia and we had to use a carriage drawn by two horses to get to the centre. The railway line passed through one of our fields where the train always had a short stop.

As children during the watermelon season we stood there carrying a yellow melon or a watermelon to sell to the passengers. Most if not all the children managed to sell one or two things. I never managed to sell a single item. I have always wondered why. Perhaps it was because I wore shoes.

People travelled from village to village on donkeys or mules usually to sell their produce or to purchase other items. As a child, I remember people who came from the mountains to sell wine and vinegar. One of them was a little strange, not very clever, but shrewd; he was red haired. He came from Kyperounda on two beautiful mules and he brought wine in two or three well-treated animal skins and vinegar in a smaller skin container. They sold the wine with a metal measure called a quarter, which contained about four and a half litres in today's terms. In those days the accepted measure was the oke. The wine seller would open one of the wine skin's legs, very carefully pour out the wine and tie it quickly so that no wine would be wasted.

The other regular visitor was Hatjigeorkis from the beautiful village of Lapithos. He was, compared to the red haired man, a gentleman. He brought us lemons, years before citrus were cultivated in our area and he brought us carob honey, which was very welcome by everybody, especially the children. My grandmother would take the lemons, the ones he brought round November; she would put them in a big cane basket in layers of straw. She would sprinkle some barley on top. Every few days she would throw some water over the barley; it would sprout, grow and keep the lemons fresh.

Both these men, like all the salesmen who came to the village, stayed at my grandmother's. Their excuse was that the house was near the coffee shops and there were plenty of stables with free straw for the animals. They only paid for the barley; a wooden bed somewhere in the house, but above all a welcoming smile and a free plate of whatever she had cooked was always offered to them. If this surprises you, in a village without hotels or inns, one had to rely on people's hospitality. I think most of us in the family inherited this trait of looking after people.

Until now I have only written of work. My grandparents always had a fair amount of entertainment in the village, such as going to weddings, going to fairs, and visiting churches and monasteries. I remember during my childhood, on special days, like the Sunday before lent, the dichoro was full of people, having dinner, drinking and having a good time. I remember watching my grandfather dancing with a glass on his head. It was so typical of his nature.

I understand from my mother that my grandmother was a very good dancer. I can believe it, judging from her figure and her movements. I never saw her dance, as she never danced after she lost her third daughter at the age of twelve. I was about one year old. These are only a few of the events in the life of my grandmother and the people around her, and some small glimpses into her character.

Unfortunately I cannot tell her story as it should be told. I can only say that every time I think of her, her habits and her attitude to life, I feel blessed for having had the chance to start my life near her. She was bedridden for about six months and looked after by her two daughters. In September 1951, I had started my teaching career in the nearby town of Morphou, so I visited her every weekend. When I visited she never ever complained, instead she kept telling me that she prayed to God that I have good luck, meaning that she prayed I would find a good husband. She kept her interest in everything that went on in the house, whether the saucepans were well scrubbed, whether a chicken or a pair of pigeons should be killed for dinner, as her daughters their families and the people who worked for them were having their dinner there. She kept an independent mind until the end. She decided to divide the land they possessed when she realised that the end was near. They talked it over and they decided what to give each daughter and they made it clear to my uncle that their decision was final. She died in June 1952, quietly without any agony at the age of seventy.

My grandfather went to live with my parents; he died in 1956, a few weeks after my elder daughter was born. His last moments were very moving. He asked my mother to go and sit near him and send for my father, my husband and myself. He had no fear or agony of mind. Death was a continuation of life. He told my mother, 'This is God's blessed hour, look your mother is sitting there waving to me...'.

A woman making a paneri (mat) with wheat stems

CHAPTER 3 - THE WASH DAY

In the days I am writing about, people in Cyprus and especially in the villages did not have the facilities to make wash day a little easier and the results somehow satisfactory. They had to invent ways and means. To be fair, the Cypriot villager was very ingenious. Strictly speaking the washday was two days and not one.

My grandmother, who was a very methodical woman, would collect the clothes on one day, sort them and soak them in the natural stone sinks. She would then scrub any stains and squeeze them tightly. Then she would place them very carefully in sturdy baskets braided in cane. She had a system: she would place the black clothes at the bottom of the basket and then she would put in the coloured ones which did not run. As most of their clothes were hand woven she was in a position to know which had fast colours. She would then place the lighter colours and then the white ones. On top she would place an old piece of material probably from an old sheet, which had to be of a fast colour. On top of this material, called the stactopanni meaning "wood-ash material" they would place ash from the oven. Whenever she fired the wood oven to bake the bread, just before she put the larger pieces of wood and the dry branches in, she would take the wood ash out, place it in an old metal container and save it for the wash day. On wash day she would sieve the ash to get rid of unburnt wood fragments and any other foreign matter and then place it on the stactopanni. Stactos means wood ash and panni is material.

Now she was ready to start the washing. She started pouring cold water on the stactopanni. In the meantime she would get the wood ash from the kitchen fireplace where better pieces of wood, like olive wood and olive branches were used, sieve it, place it in an old pithari and pour hot water over it. This is the wood ash water, the alousiva. She would then get more water from the well and fill the big copper pot and start heating it. She would continue to pour water over the clothes, first cold then warm and in the end boiling water from the big pot. At the same time she would get some water from the pithari where the wood ash was added to soften the water and pour it in the big pot. She would continue to pour water on the clothes almost all night. In the morning she and my mother would start the washing. They used the ordinary green soap.

In those days there were no detergents but with their ingenuity they managed to get excellent results and clothes which smelled good, as my grandmother would always put some bay leaves on the stactopanni or some leaves of sweetly smelling plants like rosemary.

They must have found out about wood ash as a cleansing agent by trial and error just as people once found out how cheese could be made or how bread could be produced. For wood ash contains a lot of Soda (Sodium Carbonate) and Potash (Potassium Carbonate). These two substances soften hard water, which means that they get rid of Calcium and Magnesium salts.

This was the big wash that they undertook every two or three weeks as they needed a lot of time and plenty of wood. This reminds me of our next-door neighbour who would come, every time my mother was going to start the big wash, with a huge bundle of clothes to do her wash where there was plenty of hot water. Life was difficult for the village women whose husbands did not bother to provide the wood for the oven or the kitchen fire. I must explain here that every week, usually on the Saturday, they would have the weekly wash after they had their bath.

Things were different in the mountains. I have first hand experience from the village of Kalopanayiotis in Marathassa, where my parents spent most of the summer holidays. The women would do the washing in the river not with their hands but with their feet in a rhythmic way. The waters in that area are very soft, containing no calcium or magnesium salts. After the washing was finished they would place the squeezed clothes in a cane basket that they carried to their home on their backs. The road was usually uphill and it was the easiest way to carry it. I do not know if any women still do this but I am sure that some miss the fun of doing things in company and chatting at the same time, and, to be fair, the excellent results.

CHAPTER 4 - THE BLESSING OF VEGETABLES

I don't think we really appreciate the abundance and variety of cheap fresh vegetables we have here in Cyprus. As an older Cypriot, I had the privilege of living in a village at a time when everything was seasonal. The squashes came with the watermelons and marked the beginning of summer. The villagers treasured the vegetables that they planted along the edges of the watermelon fields because they knew they wouldn't have another crop until the following summer. The housewives used to hang the ladies fingers on threads to dry them, to use in the winter. Some squashes were stored for winter use. They had many ways of cooking them without recipes: they just used what they had with love and respect. The aubergines were fried in slices to accompany fried sliced tomatoes. Sometimes to make them go further they sautéed them with onions, added chunks of tomatoes, left them to cook for a while, then added some water and rice. The ladies- fingers were fried and small potatoes, small onions and tomatoes were added. Today I cook ladies fingers in the oven to avoid less healthy frying. Often, aubergines and ladies fingers were cooked with meat. In restaurants, aubergines were cooked with lamb, and ladies fingers with chicken.

An unusual vegetable is the gourd. In some parts of Cyprus, Paphos for example, they don't use it a lot. The gourd is peeled, fried lightly, stuffed with rice, minced meat and herbs and cooked in the pan or in the oven. During fasting, on the two weeks of August (until the day of the Assumption of the Virgin Mary) however, it was peeled, sautéed with onion and left to release its water. Tomato juice was then added and it was left to cook. Later more water and then rice was added to make a good dish for the days you wanted to avoid meat or it could be used to accompany a roast.

Tomatopasta was made to preserve tomatoes for winter use. Tomatoes were cut in small pieces, left for a few days to ferment, then sieved in a colander and left to drip through muslin. After this, plenty of salt was added, and the mixture was stored in jars. People still make this, and you can often find jars of home made tomatopasta for sale in fruitarias today.

We used to take some things for granted, like the little tomatoes that ripened on the plants after they had been lifted to make way for the next crop. My Grandmother would hang the plants over the wall to ripen in the sun, and extend the season a little. Sometimes they would shrink, but to us they were perfect. Perhaps, this is the way the famous 'Italian sun dried tomatoes' originated.

With the first rains of autumn the wild vegetables come out in the fields and the hills. There are a great variety of them. 'Horta tou kambou' they are of high quality, full of flavour and fragrance. The village women welcomed them, and boiled them with pulses, black-eyed beans, haricot beans and dried broad beans to make an interesting and nourishing dish. These vegetables can be boiled on their own and served with olive oil and lemon juice served hot or cold, eaten on their own or can accompany meat or fish. In Greece, during the German occupation, the use of these vegetables saved many lives. The wild spinach you find in abundance in the fields is superior in aroma to the one you buy in the market. It can be cooked on its own or combined with meat or rice to make spinach rice pilau, (spanakorizo). The aroma and flavour of the wild vegetables differs from place to place. For example, I was once offered small spinach pies in one of the Cape Andreas villages; the spinach was collected from near the beach. I shall never forget the taste of that food.

Broad beans are widely used in Cyprus, cooked in their pods while

42

they are young and tender though this period is very short. When the pods become too tough shell the beans. They are particularly good combined with artichokes.

In those days people cooked what they produced. Today this is known as the Mediterranean diet.

Nowadays we have fassolaki all the year round. At the time I am writing about, fassolaki came out only once or twice a year. The farmers planted it round the potato fields or the field with the haricot beans.

RECIPE 1 FASSOLAKI ME TO KREAS (FRESH BEANS WITH MEAT)

INGREDIENTS

- ❑ 4-6 pieces meat or chicken.
- ❑ 1 kg fresh beans.
- ❑ A few carrots.
- ❑ 4-6 small round potatoes to make the dish go further.
- ❑ 4-6 small onions.
- ❑ Cooking oil.
- ❑ Ripe tomatoes grated or finely chopped.
- ❑ Optional: courgettes, globe artichokes, and green peppers, according to the season.

METHOD

1. Prepare the beans, carrots, potatoes etc.
2. Fry the meat lightly and remove from the pan.
3. Sauté the beans, onions, carrots and potatoes (not the courgettes, they cook very quickly).
4. Add the meat and the seasoning.
5. Add the ripe tomatoes, either finely chopped or as juice, cook for five to ten minutes, and add some water.
6. About half an hour before it is finished, add the courgettes.

I often add stuffed vine leaves to this dish with the courgettes.

THE POTATO.

The Potato is one of the most versatile foods in the kitchen. In the village house in most areas of Cyprus it was there to be used at all times. In Cyprus farmers planted potatoes twice a year, at the beginning of August and the end of January or the beginning of February. For this last crop the tubers were imported from Ireland. This crop was harvested in May or June and exported to the UK, Germany and other European countries. These are known as summer potatoes, and they are used as seed as well. The other crop was harvested in late October, November or even December, weather permitting. These days the planting times are not so rigid.

The women who followed the oxen to collect the potatoes went home with a basket full of potatoes every evening. This was on top of their wages, so they made sure they took a big basket with them. To my knowledge, this custom persists today in the potato growing area. Every home, rich or poor, had plenty of potatoes for the whole season.

What I remember vividly is the pleasure we derived by picking some small fresh potatoes from the ridges, where the new plants were growing and the potatoes we had at home were rather old. We, the farmer's children, were the first to enjoy the new potatoes. We would remove some soil from round the potato plants, take out a few tubers and put the soil back. Those potatoes were delicious.

The potato can be cooked in so many ways; boiled, fried, baked, roasted or added to a dish to make it go further. When my grandchildren come from London, they always ask to have chips for their lunch accompanied by fried halloumi, egg and lountza. While my grandchildren from the States ask for French fries, and wonder how 'Yiayia' can cook 'Macdonald's' French Fries.

The village women who came in from the fields tired and hungry or children who came home from school with healthy appetites would very quickly fry some potatoes cut in big chunks to satisfy their hunger. They could add onion rings, olives, or a tomato in small pieces. Or they would fry some eggs and halloumi to make a whole meal. Every household would develop their own ways of cooking potatoes, but some ways became traditional, for example, 'Potatoes Yiahni' a poor man's meal. Yiahni is the Cypriot equivalent of the British stew.

RECIPE 2 PATATES YIAHNI (A POOR MAN'S MEAL)

INGREDIENTS

- ❑ 1 kg potatoes.
- ❑ ½ cup oil (if a little olive oil is included, the dish has more flavour).
- ❑ 1 onion.
- ❑ ½ -1 cup celery in smoll pieces if available.
- ❑ 1 small tin tomatoes, or fresh tomatoes and some tomato paste.
- ❑ 3/4 cup rice.
- ❑ Seasoning – salt. pepper, ground cumin.
- ❑ Water to cook.

METHOD

1. Peel, wash and cut the potatoes the size of a small egg.
2. Fry the onion very lightly.
3. Add the potatoes and sauté.
4. Add the celery and sauté along with the potatoes.
5. Add the pureed tomatoes, the tomato paste dissolved in a little water, and leave to cook for five to ten minutes.
6. Add the water and let the potatoes cook. Season with salt and pepper.
7. When the potatoes are half cooked, add the washed rice. If it is necessary add more water before adding the rice.
8. When the dish is finished, add the ground cumin.

On Saturdays, when they baked bread in the outside oven, they would bake some potatoes in their skins, along with some eggs, in the hot ashes. This, with some freshly baked bread and plenty of olive oil would make a lovely evening meal.

On Sundays, when the women would light their wood oven, to cook their meat or chicken with potatoes, they would ask their relatives, friends or neighbours to bring their food to be cooked. Everyone knew what was cooking as the aroma filled the neighbourhood.

RECIPE 3 PATATES ANTINACTES (TOSSED POTATOES)

INGREDIENTS
- 1-1½ kg small new potatoes
- 1 litre cooking oil.
- ½ cup dry red wine.
- 2 tablespoons crushed coriander.
- Salt and pepper.

METHOD
1. Choose small new potatoes, wash them and scrub them with a brush.
2. Drain them well.
3. Crush them lightly.
4. Heat the oil in a deep pan and add the potatoes.
5. When they are browned, pour off the oil.
6. Add the wine and the crushed coriander, cover the saucepan and shake the pan tossing the potatoes, (antinactes)
7. If necessary add a little more wine to prevent them from burning.
8. Add salt and pepper.

COLOCASSI ESCULERITA (KNOWN AS COLOCASSI)

Many people think that colocassi is related to the potato. It is not. The potato is a tuber, whilst colocassi is a root. The potato was imported from America. Colocassi has been growing in the Middle East for hundreds of years.Colocassi is a beautiful plant with long wide leaves. In Cyprus it was grown in the Cape Peninsula, in Morphou and in Paphos.

In the villages forty or fifty years ago, colocassi was highly valued, people could only buy it when they visited the small town next to their village or when another villager came round with a donkey loaded with vegetables. In later years a van took the place of the donkey.

On Sundays the housewife would kill a chicken and use the wings. legs, neck and liver to combine with the colocassi and boil the rest of the chicken to use as broth for pasta, usually home made. In this way she produced two meals for her family. Colocassi is usually cooked with pork or chicken, but during fasting it is cooked on its own and some rice is added about half an hour before the dish is finished to give it more taste and make it go further.

PREPARATION OF COLOCASSI.

(1) Peel colocassi, never wash it, and wipe it if necessary.

(2) Cut into small pieces. Colocassi should be cut in a special way. Take a small sharp knife; start cutting small pieces, and half way through cutting begin to crack it away. This exposes more tissues and pores, which allows the root to cook more easily. This is called the 'cracked colocassi,' or 'Tsakristo,' in Greek, to differentiate it from colocassi kapamas, which is cut and cooked in a different way.

RECIPE 4 CRACKED COLOCASSI

INGREDIENTS
- ❑ *1 – 1 ½ kg colocassi.*
- ❑ *1 kg pork or chicken pieces.*
- ❑ *½ cup cooking oil with some olive oil.*
- ❑ *1 – 2 cups celery.*
- ❑ *Grated tomato or tomato juice, and some tomato paste, if you have it.*
- ❑ *Juice of 2 – 3 lemons.*
- ❑ *Water, salt and pepper.*
- ❑ *Stuffed vine leaves, optional but desirable.*

METHOD
1. *Prepare the colocassi as directed above.*
2. *Pour the oil into the pan.*
3. *Fry the pieces of meat lightly and lift from the pan.*
4. *Put all the colocassi in the pan stirring gently; return the meat to the pan.*
5. *Add the celery pieces and stir.*
6. *Add plenty of tomato juice and tomato paste.*
7. *Let it simmer for five to ten minutes*
8. *Add enough water to almost cover the food. After it boils, add the lemon juice.*
9. *Season with salt and pepper.*
10. *Taste. A lemony colocassi is better.*
11. *After about forty-five minutes, add the stuffed vine leaves and cover with a plate to keep them in place.*

METHOD

1. *Colocassi is cut into slices, not cracked, and soaked or marinated in dry red wine.*
2. *The meat, pork or chicken is fried lightly.*
3. *Colocassi is fried several pieces at a time.*
4. *Meat and colocassi are put back in the pan.*
5. *The wine in which the colocassi was marinated is added to the pan. It is then left for five to ten minutes to simmer.*
6. *The necessary water is added. It is seasoned and left to cook.*

ANGINARA - CYNARA SCOLYMUS - THE GLOBE ARTICHOKE.

I love it when the globe artichoke is in season because it can be used in such a variety of ways as a first course or a main dish. The artichoke is rich in vitamins A, B and C, and in carbohydrates. The plant is native to the Mediterranean, but today it is cultivated in many countries, not only those with a temperate climate.

In Cyprus there are several varieties of Artichoke. The early white artichoke is known as the 'Kiti,' because it is mostly cultivated in the village of Kiti near Larnaca. It appears in the market around November. It is long-stemmed, about 30-45 cm and sold individually. They are quite tender but dearer than the other varieties. The late artichoke, which comes from the same area, is harvested in February. It has a shorter stem and is sold by weight.

In the village of Mammari, not far from Nicosia, on the green line, the black artichoke is cultivated. It has a dark violet colour, comes out in April, it is tender and tastier.

In Paphos at the same time and through May, one finds the local artichoke, which is cultivated around the vineyards. This artichoke has a round head and a dark violet colour. I can also remember a small wild artichoke, which used to be brought to my village near Morphou when I was a child. The village women used to pick it from the countryside where it grew wild on the low hills. This area is occupied now and I don't know if this variety still exists there, it had a very small head with thorns; I believe a similar artichoke is found in France and is considered a delicacy.

ANGINARA RECIPES - GLOBE ARTICHOKE RECIPES.

- **Raw artichokes** – Anginares Omes. Raw artichokes are served as part of the meze table in Cyprus, Greece, Lebanon and Turkey. Young globe artichokes are chosen and three or four layers of leaves are removed. Trim off the section of each leaf and cut around the base. Cut each artichoke into squares and scoop the chokes with a spoon or sharp vegetable knife. Serve with lemon juice and lemon wedges.

- **Artichokes with eggs.** Choose tender artichokes and prepare them as above. Cut in small pieces, fry lightly and pour off most of the oil. Add the lightly beaten eggs and cook them until they are set. This dish can be served on a meze table or cooked as a snack.

RECIPE 6 ARTICHOKES WITH BROAD BEANS. ANGINARES ME KOUKIA

Artichokes are often married with broad beans in the Mediterranean. This dish can be served hot as a main dish, or cold as a starter.

INGREDIENTS
- *4-6 large globe artichokes.*
- *Juice of two or three lemons.*
- *1 kg broad beans in their pods.*
- *5-6 spring onions finely chopped.*
- *3-4 tablespoons olive oil.*
- *3 tablespoons chopped parsley.*
- *Salt and pepper.*

METHOD

METHOD

1. Prepare the artichokes as described above.

2. Rub each artichoke with a cut lemon and drop it into a bowl of water acidified with the juice of a lemon.

3. Cut around the pods of the broad beans to remove the strings or shell them.

4. Soften the spring onion in the oil for two or three minutes then add the remaining lemon juice and the rest of the ingredients.

5. Cover with water and simmer until they are tender.

Another way, more often used in Cyprus, is to cook the beans in boiling water in their pods with the artichokes. Remove them from the water and place in a bowl. Sprinkle them with a good tablespoon of flour and three tablespoons of vinegar. Return them to the saucepan where you have already softened some spring onions and garlic. Cook for a few minutes and serve.

RECIPE 7 ARTICHOKES FILLED WITH SPINACH (FLORENTINE) ANGINARES ME SPANACHI

INGREDIENTS

❏ *8 globe artichokes.*
❏ *2 bundles spinach.*
❏ *50 g butter.*
❏ *1 cup sauce béchamel with grated cheese and yolks of eggs. (Sauce Mornay.)*
❏ *25 g grated cheese.*
❏ *Salt and pepper.*

METHOD

Boil the artichokes until they are tender. Boil the spinach or sauté with some butter. Press the spinach to get rid of the excess liquid. You can enrich the spinach with some fetta cheese or some white sauce or both. Fill the artichokes with the spinach and cover with

51

the sauce. Sprinkle with the cheese and a little butter. Place in the oven for a short time. They can be served as an accompaniment or as a first course. Another variation is to fill the artichokes with sauce Bolognaise, cover them with sauce Mornay, and sprinkle with grated cheese and bake in the oven.

RECIPE 8 ARTICHOKES A LA POLITA (ANGINARES A LA POLITA)

INGREDIENTS
- 4-6 artichokes, whole or cut in pieces.
- 4-6 small potatoes.
- 2 cups peas.
- 2 carrots sliced.
- 2-4 spring onions.
- Half a cup oil, (a fifty – fifty mix of olive oil and cooking oil.)
- 2 tablespoons lemon juice according to taste.
- 1 level tablespoon flour.
- Salt and pepper.
- Water.

METHOD
1. Sauté the vegetables with the spring onions.
2. Add the flour and stir well.
3. Add the lemon juice, cover the pan and leave for two minutes on low heat.
4. Add the water and leave to cook. Stir or shake the pan from time to time.

These are only a few recipes. With some imagination the housewife can produce her own. The Cypriot housewife cooks the artichoke with potatoes and meat in a stew or adds them to green beans and meat, or finishes them with an egg and lemon sauce, (avgolermo.) I always try to freeze some artichokes since they freeze so well.

Later on, during the 1950s, in my village, and in the neighbouring villages, the farmers grew carrots and beetroot along with the more traditional produce such as citrus fruit. These were exported to Europe by the Potato Board, with great success. There was plenty of work for everybody, as it was labour intensive, and the young girls worked until late at night to pack them in red net bags. The people learned to eat carrots, which were previously unknown to the villagers, and even to incorporate them into their cooking.

RECIPE 9 CARROT CAKE

INGREDIENTS
- 1 cup sugar.
- Just under 1 cup vegetable oil.
- 3 eggs.
- 2 cups flour.
- 1 ½ teaspoons ground cinnamon.
- 1 good teaspoon baking soda.
- 1 tablespoon brandy optional.
- 1 tablespoon orange water if available.
- ½ teaspoon salt.
- 3/4 teaspoon ground nutmeg.
- 3 cups shredded carrots.
- 1 cup coarsely chopped nuts.

METHOD
1. Heat oven to 175 C.
2. Grease and flour one large and one small loaf tins.
3. Cream oil and sugar together and add the eggs gradually.
4. Stir in the flour, which has been sieved with baking soda, salt, cinnamon and the nutmeg.
5. Stir in the carrots and nuts.

6. Pour the mixture into the loaf tins and bake for 40 – 45 minutes until a skewer comes out clean.

For Apple Cake substitute 3 cups chopped cooking apples for the carrots.

CHAPTER 5 - BLESSING OF THE CITRUS FRUTS

Cyprus has been famous for its citrus fruits for many years. Historically, the citrus growing areas were the towns of Famagusta and Morphou. Later, there was a boom in the price of citrus fruit as they were exported to Western and Eastern Europe. There was a tremendous increase in citrus plantations and Cyprus had a very good income from the sale of the fruit. At the same time, new varieties were cultivated. Originally the Jaffa Variety was the main fruit. (Israel had registered the name 'Jaffa' so we couldn't call it just 'Jaffa') The late ripening Valencias were then cultivated; they had the advantage of being ripe two months later than the Jaffa and sold better. After the Valencias, a new variety, the Washington Navel, which ripens even earlier than the Jaffa, was introduced. These are very aromatic and juicy oranges.

Today, we enjoy many kinds of citrus; there are a tremendous variety of oranges, grapefruits, mandarins, seville oranges, lemons and sweet lemons, and their nutritive value is becoming common knowledge. The essential oils, mandarin, neroli (orange blossom) grapefruit and pergamot are used in aromatherapy. Indeed, neroli oil is one of the most expensive oils to produce since it requires so much blossom to make a small quantity.

There are two rootstocks that are suitable for growing citrus trees in Cyprus, the Seville Orange and the Sweet Lemon. The seeds of these are planted, and when the saplings have reached a few feet tall, they are transplanted and then later grafted with whatever variety is needed. Today, if the grower wishes, he can either do this himself, or he can buy ready grafted trees from nurseries in pots.

Some years ago, whenever you visited a Cypriot home, you were always served some kind of preserved fruit in syrup 'glyko' in Greek, (pronounced 'gleeko'). Fruits such as Seville orange, pergamot, green walnut, cherry, figs, or even vegetables like carrot and aubergine are preserved in syrup as glyko. Every housewife, rich or poor, would prepare several kinds of 'glykos' to keep to offer to guests. She would serve it accompanied by a glass of water, which had been kept cool in an earthenware jug, on a tray covered with a handmade tray cloth. The glyco was served on individual plates and eaten with tiny silver forks or spoons, according to the type and the daughter of the house was expected to perform this ceremony.

Citrus fruits are preserved in many interesting ways. Here are some recipes.

RECIPE 10 CITRUS FRUIT PEEL GLYCO

This is easy to make, inexpensive, and useful in fruitcakes.

INGREDIENTS
- ❑ *10 seville oranges or pergamots.*
- ❑ *1 – 1½ kg sugar.*
- ❑ *Juice of two lemons.*

METHOD
1. *Wash the fruit.*
2. *Grate the fruit on a fine grater, removing only the zest.*
3. *Cut the peel in quarters before removing it from the fruit. (Keep the flesh of the fruit for making squash or perhaps jelly marmalade.)*
4. *Roll up the peel quarters and tie them with a piece of thread to keep them in shape.*
5. *Put the pieces of peel in a saucepan and bring to the boil. Throw the hot water away and add cold water. Put a plate on top of the peel to keep it under the water.*

6. Change the water morning and evening. Boil once more.
7. After three to five days, boil the peel. If the peel is still bitter, throw the hot water away, add fresh water and boil again. Cool immediately.
8. Test to see if the peel is tender. If you like it soft, boil it until you get it tender enough for your taste. I prefer it a little crunchy myself.
9. Take off the thread and return the peel to the saucepan.
10. Add the sugar and lemon juice.
11. Leave overnight until the sugar starts to melt a little, then boil rapidly. You may find that you need to add one or two tablespoons of water before boiling the mixture.
12. Test to see if the 'Glyco' has set, using the same method as you would for marmalade.
13. Leave to cool, place in sterilised jars, and cover.

Grapefruit Glyco is made in the same way, but you don't need to roll the peel, just cut it in whatever shapes you fancy.

HOW TO MAKE A SQUASH.

RECIPE 11 SEVILLE ORANGE, LEMON OR PERGAMOT

1. Wash the fruit and grate some zest from the rind of the fruit
2. Squeeze the fruit, and then add some zest to the juice.
3. Leave for a few hours, then strain through muslin.
4. Measure the juice and add equal quantities of sugar by volume.
5. Stir and leave for a few hours, stirring from time to time.
6. When the sugar is completely dissolved, pour the squash into sterilised bottles.
7. Store in the refrigerator.

Recipe 12 How to make a Lemon Squash without Preservative

INGREDIENTS; *these are measured by volume, for example,*
- ❑ *15 cups lemon juice,*
- ❑ *15 cups sugar.*
- ❑ *Zest of a few lemons and pergamot if you have it.*
- ❑ *Dark bottles.*
- ❑ *New corks*

Method
1. *Choose good, sound lemons.*
2. *Wash the lemons and scrub them if necessary.*
3. *Grate the zest of some lemons.*
4. *Squeeze the lemons, add the lemon zest, and leave to macerate for ten to fifteen minutes.*
5. *Strain the juice through muslin.*
6. *In the meantime, make the syrup.*
7. *Put the sugar in a good thick pan and add three cups of the lemon juice if you are using a fifteen to fifteen ratio. Adjust the amount if your quantities are different.*
8. *Stir well.*
9. *Place on the cooker and heat slowly stirring all the time.*
10. *When it boils, take it off the heat and leave it to cool.*
11. *Pour the strained juice onto the syrup stirring all the time.*
12. *Strain again through the muslin into a clean pot*
13. *Pour into dark clean bottles, which have been sterilised in a slow oven. (About 150˚C)*
14. *Seal with corks, new if possible, which have been boiled for a few minutes.*
15. *It is advisable to seal the corks, by turning the bottle upside down and dipping the cork into melted paraffin wax.*
16. *Store in a cool place. If you keep everything scrupulously*

clean, the squash will keep for more than a year. Once the bottle is opened, keep it in a refrigerator.

Orange squash is made in exactly the same way:

INGREDIENTS
- ❑ *10 cups orange juice, preferably from Valencia oranges.*
- ❑ *2 cups lemon juice.*
- ❑ *3 cups lemon juice for the syrup.*
- ❑ *15 cups sugar.*

RECIPE 13 A YELLOW CAKE WITH CLEAR ORANGE FILLING

For the cake.

INGREDIENTS
- ❑ *2 cups flour*
- ❑ *1 cup sugar*
- ❑ *½ cup shortening*
- ❑ *1 cup milk and orange juice*
- ❑ *3 ½ tsp. baking powder*
- ❑ *3 eggs*
- ❑ *some Orange zest*

METHOD
1. *Cream the fat and sugar.*
2. *Add the eggs one by one and continue beating.*
3. *Add the flour alternating with the liquid.*
4. *Fold in the orange zest.*
5. *Grease and flour two round pans and bake in a moderate oven at about 175˚C. for approximately 40 – 45 minutes, or until the cakes pull away from the sides of the tin, or a skewer inserted comes out clean.*
6. *Take out of the oven and when it is cool, sandwich with clear*

orange filling. I put the filling over the top of the cake as well instead of using another icing.

For the filling:
- [ ] 1 cup orange juice.
- [ ] 2/3 cup sugar.
- [ ] 1/4 cup cornflour.
- [ ] A pinch of salt.
- [ ] 2 tablespoons butter.
- [ ] 2 tablespoons orange zest.
- [ ] 2 tablespoons lemon juice.

METHOD
1. In a thick saucepan mix the orange juice, sugar and cornflour.
2. Beating all the time, bring it to the boil until it starts to thicken.
3. Remove from the heat and add the butter, the orange zest and the lemon juice. Heat until the required consistency is reached.
4. Cool, stirring all the time.
5. Pour onto the cakes, spread carefully and sandwich together.

I like to make this cake in March when the orange trees are in bloom, and decorate my tray with orange blossom.

RECIPE 14 CLEAR LEMON FILLING

INGREDIENTS
- [ ] 3/4 cup water.
- [ ] 3/4 cup sugar.
- [ ] 3 tablespoons cornflour.
- [ ] A pinch of salt.
- [ ] 1 tablespoon butter.
- [ ] 2 tablespoons lemon zest.
- [ ] 1/3 cup lemon juice.

Method as for orange filling. This can be used on a lemon cake.

RECIPE 15 PASTRY WITH ORANGE JUICE

suitable for olive pies

INGREDIENTS

- ❑ *2 cups pastry flour.*
- ❑ *1 cup all purpose flour.*
- ❑ *Just under ½ cup cooking oil.*
- ❑ *A pinch of salt.*
- ❑ *3 teaspoons baking powder.*
- ❑ *As much orange juice as it takes to make a soft pliable dough.*
- ❑ **Filling**
- ❑ *1-1 ½ cups finely chopped black olives.*
- ❑ *1 small onion very finely chopped.*
- ❑ *A little mint.*
- ❑ *½ cup chopped coriander if available.*
- ❑ *1 tablespoon olive oil.*

METHOD

1. Sieve the flour with the baking powder.

2. Add the oil and rub it into the flour.

3. Add the orange juice gradually to the flour and mix until a soft and pliable dough is obtained.

4. Roll out the dough.

5. Cut the dough with a pastry cutter.

6. Place the filling in the corner of the circle.

7. Fold the pastry in such a way as to make a roll.

8. Place on greased trays and bake in a moderate oven at about 175˚C..

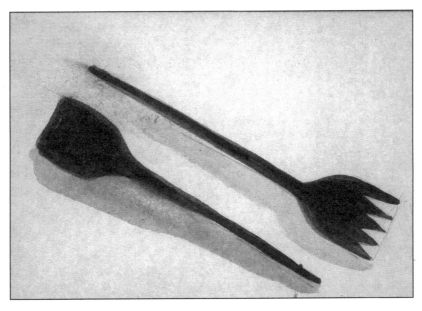

Wooden shovels - plain and teethed necessary on the threshing floor

CHAPTER 6 - FARMING, WATER, AND FLAX

Farming, as it was practised when I was very young, was in the hands of God. It was extremely hard work, quite frequently not very productive and perhaps often not very efficient. It relied so much on the weather, mainly on the rain, as there was no other way to water the crops. The farmers looked at the sky and tried to predict the weather. They prayed for a good crop. I remember the third of November in particular as it is devoted to Ayios Georghios, the saint of sowing. I chose to sleep at my Grandmother's. She would wake us up and ask us to kneel, cross ourselves in the way the Greek Orthodox do, take three handfuls of the seed and put it in the sack. After that my Grandparents would add the amount of seed needed. They believed that as children we had no sins so God would listen to us.

During my Grandfather's farming days, wheat, barley and cumin were cultivated. My Grandfather was a very hardworking man. When he was a young man he had worked in the Monasteries of Kykko, in Avlona, where the monastery owned a lot of land, and at the monastery of Archangelos. In those days it was a few miles outside Nicosia, now it is part of the city. So he had the chance to live next to a monk, who was an educated man and who was very kind to my Grandfather. In this way, he had a taste of the wider world outside the village. It was something that the other young men did not have the chance to do. He used this knowledge later, years after he got married.

He realised that if they wanted to cultivate more crops they had to have water. So he persuaded a number of people who owned enough land to form a company to try to find water. With the knowledge he had gained whilst working at the monastery, he went to Lakatamia, where he met one of the well diggers. He persuaded him to come and work in the village. My mother does not remember very much about this but she tells me that the well digger and his assistants were given meals on a weekly basis by each member of the company as there were no restaurants or any other facilities.

Each family baked their bread every week; if their bread was finished they would borrow from a neighbour or relation. If the loaf was not very fresh it was less palatable so it lasted longer. In those days there was only one shop in the village, owned by Karapavlos, one of my father's uncles. He sold wine, vinegar, perhaps cooking oil and sometimes salted cod, sardines and kippers. It was a time when people ate what they produced, adding to it plenty of wild vegetables they picked from the fields. Quite often they picked from the fields of people who had more.

So the well digger came with his assistants. My mother has suddenly remembered that his name was Michaelas. They chose a spot near the river to start digging. They found water, then dug more wells which they connected together with tunnels. They did not connect them to the first well with the water, so that they would not be soaked or drowned while they worked. Many villagers, even children, worked, drawing the gravel out of the wells in specially prepared straw baskets. Some villagers worked for money, some worked instead of paying taxes, and some worked as a contribution to their membership of the newly formed company. When they had dug enough wells and interconnecting tunnels, and the tunnel level reached that of the lower fields, they went back and connected the first well with the tunnel. So the water came to the surface through the tunnel.

Farming gradually changed. The water was running all the time. The water obviously belonged to the few who had initiated the digging and contributed the money. Every shareholder, according to his contribution, was allowed so many hours of running water every ten days. Soon, another group of villagers tried to do the same, digging near the same spot. There was a lot of fighting in the courts and finally there was an agreement. The first group compromised and the water was shared between the shareholders every fortnight. Now people were able to plant summer crops as well. Potatoes could be planted twice a year, the August crop to be harvested in November and December, and the February crop to be harvested in May or June, depending on the weather. Beans were planted as well, and in the summer the whole area was producing loads of melons and watermelons. Lorries came from all over Cyprus to buy the melons to resell in other villages. Katokopia, my husband's village, only half a mile away from mine, was famous all over Cyprus for its watermelons.

The local diet was improved as the villagers planted all kinds of vegetables in the watermelon fields; tomatoes, cucumbers, eggplant, squash and many kinds of greens. Needless to say, some of the women would load this produce on their donkeys and go to sell to the neighbouring villages, very often coming back with less than, or just over a pound for their trouble. I would like to mention here that life in the village during the watermelon season was very exciting, and on the watermelon fields more so, especially for the children.

Farming is not static. Flax and cotton were soon introduced to our village (it had been grown in parts of Cyprus in medieval times) I remember the flax flowers in one of our fields; it was magic for when there was a little breeze they seemed to be dancing. The harvesting of flax was very interesting to watch; so many people working together harmoniously, each one knowing what to do and what his neighbour has to do. Quite often huge black snakes would crawl out or lift up their heads, but the workers were not frightened, as they knew the black snakes were harmless. What I remember vividly is the food my mother took along to the field. As the harvest was after Easter, she always included red eggs and the special Easter bread, flaounes.

The flax was tied in bundles and then piled in heaps. If it looked like raining these heaps had to be covered with sheaves of barley or whatever was available. When the flax was dried, it was carried, always by donkey, to the threshing field where it was pounded to free the seeds, which were sold separately. The sheaves of flax were then carried a few miles away where it was placed in a big ditch with stagnant waters. These waters had a foul smell. Decay and fermentation were taking place in the water and, at the same time, bleaching agents were produced, which whitened and softened the flax while it soaked in the stagnant water for over a week. It was then taken out of the ditch and left for a few days to dry. When my Grandfather took the flax to the ditch which was managed by the same people every year, he would take a lot of food; so many loaves according to the number of sheaves of flax, a pot of cooked food, more food to be cooked there, olive oil, olives, halloumi, onions, even salt.. In those days, food was very important, and if you wanted a good job done, you had to feed the people who worked for you very well. I must say here that both my maternal Grandmother, and later my mother, had a very good name in that respect. When the flax was dry, it was brought back to the village on donkeys, nine sheaves, four on each side, and one on top. It was taken on the roof and left there for several days to dry completely.

It was then brought down and another lengthy process was ahead of them. Women of a certain age, familiar with the job, were employed. These women were paid according to the amount of work they produced. By today's standards it would amount to five or seven cents per hour. I must point out here that they were given three good meals a day. In the morning they were given a soup like trahanas; if it was a fasting time they had tsorvas. For supper they always had a cooked meal of pulses with wild vegetables or some home made pasta. Lunch varied according to the weather. Sometimes they would

66

ask for watermelon, bread and olives often with some dry anari. They always cooked what they had in the house or on the fields.

The first job they had was to take a bundle of flax and pound it with a specially prepared club to get rid of the bark and release the part which would later be used to make the thread. I remember this very well; it was before I went to school and I wanted to have my own club. So my grandfather had a small club made especially for me. After this process they used a special gadget made of wood, called melidja. The village carpenter made this gadget. We had several in our village house as we were planning to have a family museum with farming tools but these we lost in 1974 along with everything else in the village. Melidja was made of two pieces of wood fixed together so as to form a cavity and a third piece stuck at one end. By putting the flax in the melidja hitting it with the other piece of wood and moving it in a special way the flax was freed from most of the hard parts.

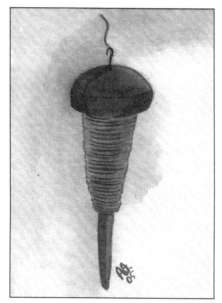

The adrakti for spinning flax, wool or cotton.

They then made the flax in special bundles of one oke, an old weight measure, equivalent to 1280 grams. These bundles were a work of art. The flax was almost ready to be made into thread. My grandmother and my mother needless to say, left the best bundles to make into thread for use in their hand weaving. Before they started to make the thread, always by hand, either with the adrakti or the roka (which was my grandmother's favourite) they

67

scraped the flax with a special scraper to get rid of the last pieces of foreign matter. To make it quite smooth they brushed it with a special brush made with the hairs taken from the neck of a pig after it was killed but before it was scraped clean.

The women made fine linen thread, which was used both in weaving and in embroidery. The men made thicker thread, which was used for making ropes or by having it woven into sacks. As a child, I remember all men, young and old alike, in the coffee shop especially on a rainy day spinning the flax on their adracta. In our village there were two people who had special looms for weaving the sacks; one was Salih, a Turkish Cypriot and the other a Greek Cypriot, Pantelas.

In the nearby village of Zodia a small factory was built to make linen thread and to weave linen cloth of different widths to satisfy the demand of the Lefkara lace industry. Special wide looms were introduced in our village and some women were trained. This home industry was flourishing.

The farmers used many parts of the flax. They sold the flax for thread. The seeds were sold, the rough parts of the flax were used to heat the oven for the weekly baking of bread, and the thin parts were mixed in the mud, which was used to cover the roofs of the house. It was very effective as the mud made with flax shreds never cracked.

Flax growing is labour intensive. With the beginning of the Second World War, many chances of work were created outside the village; the work was lighter and the money better than working with flax. In addition the farmers were encouraged to grow more food like potatoes, beans and pulses along with the cultivation of wheat and barley. All food sold at very good prices and it was in great demand. In 1942, was the year I went to Nicosia to the secondary school. Before Christmas the assistant Principal in a joking manner said to me, 'And what are you going to donate to the Christmas raffle, Zenonos?' Although I felt very shy, a village girl among many town girls, I answered very quickly. 'I can bring an oke of black eyed beans, Sir.' Funny as it might seem the beans were received with great pleasure and they were divided in three bags.

The war brought many home industries to an end, flax growing amongst them and the small factory in Zodia closed. After the war the linen material was imported from Ireland.

CHAPTER 7 - THE WATERMELON FIELDS

For years my village Arghaki and the neighbouring villages of Katokopia and Zodia cultivated melons and watermelons. Katokopia was famous for its watermelons and Zodia for a special variety of melons. Then they cultivated the fruits, relying on the rain and the water they could get from the river. The field was watered very well before they planted the seeds. Later, once they had built the chains-of-wells described in chapter 6, it became much easier to grow melons. When the field had the right humidity, the farmer would mark the furrow with oxen, mules or even donkeys. His wife or his daughter would follow to sow the seeds. After about ten days, the seeds would germinate. The wife would go and plant more seeds in any gaps. These days the farmer buys the plants ready grafted onto little squash plants to make them stronger. I may be prejudiced, but the watermelons we produce today cannot be compared in taste with the ones I remember from my childhood.

My father would choose a few really big ones to keep until Christmas. Some people would take a watermelon to church on Epiphany day, the sixth of January, which they had kept since the summer. Modern watermelon varieties do not keep as long. In the same field they would plant tomatoes, cucumbers and adjourga (similar to cucumber but much more tasty). Round the edges of the fields they would plant squashes, black-eyed beans, eggplants and French beans.

Of course, the farmers planted the watermelons for an income, but, at the same time, the watermelon growing was part of a way of life, just like the goats, that they kept for the milk and the cheese making. Very often a villager even if he did not own much land would plant watermelons to keep the family fed with fresh fruit and vegetables during the long hot summer. It also kept the children busy. If a family did not plant a watermelon field, often a neighbour or friend would call by at mid morning with a donkey-load of watermelons, melons and fresh vegetables. If you passed a watermelon field when the owner was there, he would call you to come and have some watermelon to cool you down, and give you some to take with you. If you were working near a watermelon field, the watermelon man or woman would call carrying a huge watermelon to cool you down.

During the watermelon season the village was full of life. The children had school holidays then, so they would go to the field in the morning, sometimes taking two, three or four goats with their kids. They would be responsible for looking after them, and protecting the crops from birds and passers by. They were given some food and cooking utensils, a simple frying pan, a fork and a bottle of cooking oil. They also took a bottle of oil and vinegar to make vinaigrette for their salad (ladoxido). These were placed in the shade of the squash plants.

Each morning the children would bring a basket containing some bread and an egg. All the children, boys and girls, would get together from the neighbouring fields to cook their lunch. They built a small fire between two stones and fried the vegetables they picked fresh from the field, courgettes, or tender squash, squash flowers, one or two tomatoes and in the end they would break and fry the precious egg. Sometimes they stirred and mixed it with the vegetables, sometimes they left it whole. The children ate together in a purpose built shed or under a wild mosfilo tree; these were often to be found at the end of the field. As a child, I loved these summers. It meant a great deal to me to be a member of a group, especially as I was an only child. These memories led me to create my watermelon field omelette recipe.

In the evening the father would come to the field. Sometimes he would have eaten at home, but often he would bring his supper to eat in the cool evening. He would sleep in the purpose built shed, on a wooden plank made by him or the grandfather. When the watermelons were ready, he would often rise before sunrise to cut the stems of the ripe fruit with a small sharp knife. He would move each one a little so it was easy to see which ones were cut. His wife, the neighbours, the relations and any other people who were available would help to carry the watermelons to the end of the field. An experienced farmer could tell just by looking if they were ready to be picked; if not, he would have to knock on the fruit to listen to the sound. My mother tells me that one morning my father was cutting watermelons for five hours. They would carry them in twos or threes in a sack to the end of the field and put them in a tidy heap to be covered from the strong sunlight. This I call real work.

The farmer went to the coffee shop in the centre of the village, waiting for a lorry, to sell his watermelons. Sometimes he would sell the whole heap without weighing or he would sell by weight. Often they sold very cheaply, the equivalent of a couple of cents for an oke, (1280) grams. Watermelons were weighed in huge cane baskets; one man stood in the lorry and he caught the fruit in such a way that he never missed one. I was fascinated and could not stop watching him. The man loading the lorry had to stack the fruit in such a way that they would not shift in transit. They often had to take them long distances to the mountain villages, which in those days were the fashionable resorts of Cyprus.

After the first crop was picked the field was watered so as to get as many watermelons as possible. The last crop was of very small watermelons, which we used to pick, break with our thumbs and eat. Towards the end of the harvest, a lot of fruit was taken home as in those days it was the only fruit available in the village. The very small watermelons were taken home to be fed to the goats. After this the farmer came to an agreement with a shepherd who took his flock to feed on the plants.

RECIPE 16 THE WATERMELON FIELD OMELETTE

INGREDIENTS
- ☐ *2 courgettes or 1 squash.*
- ☐ *A couple of green peppers.*
- ☐ *1 aubergine.*
- ☐ *Two tomatoes.*
- ☐ *3-4 eggs.*
- ☐ *Some cooking oil.*
- ☐ *Fresh mint and basil. (optional)*
- ☐ *Salt and pepper.*

METHOD
1. *Wash the aubergine, cut in small pieces, salt and leave for at least twenty minutes.*
2. *Wash the courgettes, cut in small pieces, fry them lightly then put them in a small colander to drain.*
3. *Do the same with the peppers.*
4. *Wash the aubergine, dry and fry in the same way.*
5. *Drain all the vegetables to remove excess oil.*
6. *Fry the tomatoes, and return all the drained vegetables to the frying pan and stir to mix.*
7. *In the meantime, break three or four eggs; add seasoning and the herbs. Pour over the vegetables and heat until the eggs are set.*

In the long hot summers the people of my village and the people of the neighbouring villages enjoyed the watermelons at all times of the day. They ate watermelon on its own to cool down; they ate watermelon with bread and halloumi for breakfast or for supper. When the wives found a watermelon with thick peel, which was quite often, they made glyco out of it.

RECIPE 17 WATERMELON PEEL GLYCO

INGREDIENTS

- ❏ 30 pieces of about 5-6 cm squares or rectangles of thick watermelon peel.
- ❏ 2/3 cup of quicklime to make lime water.
- ❏ 2 kg sugar.
- ❏ The juice of three or four lemons.
- ❏ 2 tablespoons orange blossom water.

METHOD

1. To make this glyco you have to have a really thick peel. Wash the peel well. Cut it in nice pieces of about five to six cm, either in squares or rectangles.
2. Peel the green outside of the watermelon and take away the pink flesh on the inside of the peel.
3. Dissolve the quicklime in plenty of water, filter if necessary and place the watermelon pieces in it. Leave for a couple of hours to soak.
4. Take them out and wash them very well.
5. Throw them into a pan of boiling water and leave them until the water starts boiling again.
6. Wash them in cold water and place them back in boiling water. Repeat this two or three times until the peel is tender when pierced with a needle.
7. Cool the peel very well so that it is soft but crunchy.
8. Throw the peel into cold water into which you have squeezed the lemons and leave for a couple of hours.
9. Take the pieces of peel out ,drain them well and place them in a pan with the sugar and some lemon juice.

10. After three or four hours or the following morning, add about one cup water and boil until it sets. If you like you can leave it in the pan and you boil it the following day.

11. When quite cold place the peel with the syrup into sterilized jars and cover. If you like, drain some of the pieces, roll them in sugar and dry them in the sun. In this way it is more convenient to serve.

   It is simple and cheap to make, you can fit it in your day's work, and it is very refreshing when served with a glass of cold water.

CHAPTER 8 - CHRISTMAS IN CYPRUS

When I was a child many, many years ago, Christmas was celebrated more as a religious holiday. In 1942, when I was a student in the first class of the Pancyprian Gymnasium in Nicosia, I saw my first Christmas tree. It was on the stage of the school theatre; it was beautiful; it was magic to me! It was something quite new in Cyprus. I remember listening to the late well-known painter Adamantios Diamantis telling a colleague, 'It is beautiful, but it is foreign, (xeno) to Cyprus". Nowadays, every family, rich or poor, will decorate a Christmas tree.

In many villages in Cyprus during the Christmas holidays and in some others during Easter, the young men and women amused themselves on swings, (souses). A house with a huge room (dichoro) would be chosen. It had to have an arch in the middle. A strong rope would be hung from the ceiling, two loops were tied at the ends and a strong board inserted through the loops.

The swing would take between four and six people, either young women or young men; they never sat together. On either side of the board stood a young boy who moved the swing. The young women would sit on the swing first, one group after the other. Each of the girls would take their turn in singing. There was no music except their singing voices. The songs were made up on the spot; few of them rehearsed at home. These songs are short; four lines in rhyme; interesting, spontaneous, full of feeling and often full of humour. Quite a number of studies have been published on the 'Songs of the Swings' (Trayoudhia tis Sousas), by people who studied folklore. The swing had to be put up on Sunday after church and taken down in the evening, usually this continued every Sunday until lent.

This was one of the few amusements for the young people. It was the meeting place where they would most probably choose their future fiancé. As children, we were always present, watching, listening, and discussing together. We had our own fun. Most of all, we loved Christmas. Mothers and grandmothers enjoyed the preparation of the food, the big feast and the gathering of the family.

During the twelve days of Christmas there was no fasting on Wednesdays and Fridays, as is usually the custom. Quite often, the villagers slaughtered the pig they bred at home for the occasion; so there was a lot of food, drink and fun for the relatives and friends. Most of the meat was preserved in different ways, as sausages or lountza, and the fat was rendered down into lard. They would give us the pig's bladder, which we inflated and used as a ball to play with for a while.

People, and especially children, believed that during the twelve days of Christmas until Epiphany day, the 6th of January, when 'the waters are baptised' the evil spirits (kalikantzari) are let loose to wander around the earth. We children pictured them as small creatures, dressed in black, with horns and a tail. We were afraid to walk around the village at night.

On the 5th of January, every housewife would make 'loukoumathes' (round pieces of batter deep-fried and finished in syrup). According to the tradition, she had to throw some of the newly prepared sausages with the loukoumathes on the roof of the house for the 'Kalikantzari.' She would ask the spirits to eat them and go away until the following year. Our Christmas definitely did not come from a supermarket, as so much does today. As children, we were never given, nor did we expect, toys. We made our own toys, but we were given new clothes and new shoes. There was, though, a lot of fun, love and a sense of belonging.

RECIPE 18 KOURAPIEDES (THE CYPRUS SHORT COOKIE)

A festive cookie prepared for both Christmas and Easter and very often for name days.

INGREDIENTS

- ❑ 12 ounces or 350 grams shortening. I use a small tin of spry.
- ❑ 1 cup icing sugar.
- ❑ 3 tablespoons water which has been boiled with a few cloves and a cinnamon stick.
- ❑ 2 teaspoons brandy and rose or orange water.
- ❑ 1½ teaspoons baking powder.
- ❑ As much flour as it takes to make a pliable dough, which does not stick on the palms.

METHOD

1. Cream the shortening and the icing sugar.
2. Add the liquids and the flour that has been sieved with the baking powder.
3. Add more flour until you get a pliable dough, shaping different shapes, but keeping them the same size for even baking.
4. Bake in a moderate oven about 170°C.
5. About ten minutes after you take them out of the oven, sprinkle them with icing sugar, cool and pile them in a cookie tin.

RECIPE 19 COOKIES STUFFED WITH DATES: A CHRISTMAS COOKIE

INGREDIENTS

- ❑ ½ cup milk made up by dissolving two tablespoons of sweetened milk in warm water.
- ❑ 1 packet unsalted butter. (Half a pound.)
- ❑ 2 egg yolks. Keep the whites to use later.
- ❑ ½ cup icing sugar

- 3 teaspoons baking powder
- 1 teaspoons cinnamon.
- 2 tablespoons brandy .
- As much flour as it takes to make a dough which does not stick on the palms.

For the stuffing:
- About two cups dates
- ½ cup finely chopped almonds or walnuts or both.
- Two or three pieces of pergamot or grapefruit peel glyco or any preserved peel
- About two tablespoons syrup from the glyko.
- Some cinnamon and very little grated nutmeg.
- Ground almonds to roll the cookies in.

METHOD

1. Cream the butter and the sugar
2. Add the yolks gradually beating all the time.
3. Add the flour and the warm milk alternately using the mixer on low speed.
4. Move the bowl from the mixer and knead the dough, adding a little flour if it is needed. The dough should be soft but it should not stick on the palms.
5. Either roll the dough out thinly or cut into rounds of a size you want or take walnut-sized lumps and flatten them out thinly between the palms of your hands. Traditionally these should be half moon shaped.
6. Put a heaped teaspoon stuffing in the center of each circle. Fold the other half over to make the shape of a half moon or a horseshoe and seal by pinching with a fork
7. Roll them in the egg whites and then on ground almonds to which a little cinnamon has been added.
8. Bake in a moderate oven at about 175°C.

This is a traditional Christmas cookie, prepared in most homes in Cyprus just before Christmas. Those who cannot cook it at home buy it from the local bakeries. The writer, the late Eugenia Petronda, who came from Alexandria in Egypt to live in Cyprus, gave me this recipe.

INGREDIENTS
- ❑ *1 cup cooking oil*
- ❑ *1 cup shortening-I use spry*
- ❑ *1 cup orange juice, with the zest of the orange.*
- ❑ *½ cup brandy.*
- ❑ *½ cup sugar for the dough.*
- ❑ *1 level tablespoon ground cinnamon.*
- ❑ *1 level tablespoon ground cloves. Use less if you find them very strong.*
- ❑ *1 tablespoon baking powder.*
- ❑ *As much flour as it takes to make a dough which does not stick to the palms of your hands.*

For the syrup:
- ❑ *1 cup sugar*
- ❑ *½ cup honey.*
- ❑ *1 ½ cups water.*
- ❑ *A few drops of lemon juice.*
- ❑ *A piece of cinnamon stick.*

METHOD
1. *Cream the fat and the sugar.*
2. *Gradually add all the liquid ingredients.*
3. *Add enough flour, sieved with the baking powder, the cinnamon and the ground cloves to make a pliable dough.*

4. Shape the cookies in the shape of a date.

5. Cook in a moderate oven.

6. When they are ready, place a few at a time in the boiling syrup and take them out with a ladle as soon as the syrup returns to the boil again.

7. Place them on a tray with ground almonds and or walnuts to which some sugar and cinnamon have been added.

8. Turn them around to cover them with the nuts.

9. Place them on trays until they are dry and store them in containers.

CHAPTER 9 - T'AIVASSILIOY: NEW YEAR'S DAY MEMORIES.

New Year's Day in Cyprus and within all the Greek World is known as the day of Ayios Vassilios. Ayios Vassilios was a Bishop in Caesarea and, as such, he is honoured in the Greek Orthodox Church. In the Greek folk tradition, in his worldly appearance he is the incarnation of the New Year and quite often he is synonymous with Father Christmas and therefore, as such, has become part of the Season's advertising.

In the Greek tradition Ayios Vassilios has three identities. A Traveller with a piece of writing paper in one hand and the sacred rod in the other hand A Ploughman or a sower of the Greek fields and a Prophet who could foretell the fate of poor unmarried girls.

There are many folk songs about Ayios Vassilios and his role in the seasonal celebrations. Every housewife in the villages, when she baked the sesame bread before Christmas, or if she baked again before the New Year, would make a big round sesame bread especially for New Year's Eve. This bread was called Vassilis. When she shaped the bread, she took two strips of dough. She placed them on the bread so as to make a cross, from one end of the loaf to the other end. At the point where the strips met she stabbed them together so as to make sure that a hollow would be shaped where they would place the candle. The day before the New Year the mother would clean the wheat of all foreign matter, soak it for a while and then boil it to make kolliva. The kolliva was mixed with sesame seeds, raisins, blanched almonds, and pomegranate seeds if available and served in a bowl.

On New Year's Eve the bowl with the kolliva was placed on a table in a quiet corner of the house with the special bread, Vassilis. Next to this a bottle of wine and a half full glass of wine were placed. The candle was placed on the cross formed by the two strips of dough and lit only for a short time, as they were afraid of causing fire. During the night they left lit a paraffin lamp, as most villages did not have electricity in those days, so that Ayios Vassilios would be able to visit the table without tripping over.

My grandfather would place his old leather purse on the table to be blessed by Ayios Vassilios. He always encouraged us, all the grandchildren to place our small sums of money there too. In the morning we always found a little more and we used to think that Ayios Vassilios had put it there.

The day before New Year's Day, they would pick olive tree branches to decorate windows and doors to mark the beginning of the New Year. On New Year's Eve and New Year's Day we would sit around an open fire; if there was no open fire, people would make one by placing coal in a special metal container. During the day we would pick plenty of olive tree branches. We used to take an olive tree leaf, throw it on the burning coal and sing.

Vassili, Vassilia (King)

Climb the olive tree

And show whether so and so loves me (Ayios Vassilios the prophet.)

If the leaf made a noise and gave a little jumping movement, which it usually did the answer was yes. If it just burned away quickly the answer was no and we were greatly disappointed.

Every household in the village had a number of clay pots in which water from the well was stored. These pots were covered with a whole thyme plant so that dust and insects were kept away. When the mother washed the wheat for the kolliva on the day before New

Year's Day, she would sow wheat seeds into the thyme. She would also sprinkle water on the thyme daily so as to help the seeds to germinate. When the wheat in the thyme had grown enough, about 20 cm, and the wheat in the fields started to grow, the whole thyme plant with the germinated wheat would be transplanted in the wheat field as blessing and luck.

In my family, this job was done by my grandfather, a very hard working and religious man. He would visit his different fields carrying on his shoulders his goatskin bag. (vourka). In his vourka he always carried a bottle of water, which had been blessed in church the day before Epiphany Day, January 6, and the thyme bunches with the germinated wheat. He planted the thyme and sprinkled the field with the blessed water.

When I was a child there were no other special celebrations or parties on New Year's Eve. On New Year's Day they would cook a rather older chicken (to give a good broth) which they always killed the day before. They would boil it and cook in the broth the homemade macaroni, which was sprinkled with grated halloumi or dry anari. If they expected more people they would kill a younger chicken as well and cook it with potatoes or with colocassi.

Nowadays, every household rich or poor celebrates New Year's Eve by inviting the whole family and close friends. Quite a lot of people celebrate the evening in hotels and restaurants. At midnight, on New Year's Eve or the following day after lunch, the head of the family cuts the vassilopitta. The head makes the sign of the cross with his sharp knife and marks the pieces so that everybody, starting with a piece for the poor, one for the house, one for each member of the family starting with the youngest. The members of the family who are absent get a piece kept for them. Then the guests get their slice; it is probably the only time in Cyprus hospitality that the guests come second.

These are very exciting moments especially for the children as everybody wants to win the lucky coin and hope for a happy New Year.

There are many recipes for vassilopitta. I shall give you my own. If you have a crowd you can always double it.

RECIPE 21 VASSILOPITTA

INGREDIENTS

- ❑ 1/3 cup shortening
- ❑ 1 cup sugar (a little less than one cup)
- ❑ 1 egg
- ❑ 2 cups plain flour sieved with 2½ good teaspoons baking powder
- ❑ About 2/3 cup milk and a good tablespoon of brandy
- ❑ The zest of one orange
- ❑ Enough blanched almonds to put on the cake to mark the New Year.

METHOD

1. Cream together the shortening and the sugar
2. Add the egg and beat well
3. Add some of the milk alternately with the flour, which has been sieved with the baking powder. At the same time, add the orange zest.
4. Place in a greased and floured baking tin
5. Mark out the coming year's date with the blanched almonds.
6. Bake in a moderate oven 170°C
7. While the cake is in the oven prepare the topping by mixing one or two tablespoons of shortening 2-3 tablespoons sugar, some orange zest, plenty of desiccated coconut and some milk and heat lightly.
8. About 15 minutes before the cake is finished take it out of the oven carefully and spread it with the prepared topping.
9. Put it back in the oven until it is ready.

Do not forget to include the lucky coin in a piece of greaseproof paper and place it in the mixture.

HAPPY NEW YEAR.

CHAPTER 10 - TSIKNO PEMPTY

The Thursday before the Sunday of the Apocreo is called the Tsikno Pempty or the Thursday of the smell of burning meat, as on this day the people eat and celebrate before the beginning of the long fasting begins. Every householder will prepare something very tasty on this day. In the villages and in many town homes the housewife would make her own phyllo pastry with one or several fillings and make small pies, which she would usually fry in deep fat or cook on something like a wok. Although these days, many women work they still try to mark this day; if they do not have the time or the know-how, they will buy these interesting little pies from special shops. The fillings are both savoury and sweet. Often there is the filling of grated halloumi mixed with egg and fresh or dry mint. Another filling is pork minced meat cooked with spices. A sweet filling is unsalted anari with a little sugar and cinnamon. All these are completed with nicely cooked meat dishes and in many occasions home made sausages.

RECIPE 22 BOUREKIA OR SMALL PIES

This is a festive dish - there are as many recipes as there are people. It is very popular in many countries. The fillings are either savoury such as cheese, minced meat or spinach, or sweet, like anari sweetened with a little sugar.

For the dough:
- ❏ *4 cups pastry flour*
- ❏ *1/3 cup cooking oil*
- ❏ *1 pinch salt*
- ❏ *1 small teaspoon baking powder.*
- ❏ *Warm water to mix, about 1 cupful.*

METHOD

1. Sieve the flour with the salt and the baking powder.
2. Add the oil and rub it into the flour.
3. Add water gradually, working it all the time until a soft and pliable dough is formed
4. Allow the dough to rest for about an hour.
5. Roll the dough out on a lightly floured board with a floured rolling pin or with a pastry machine. The dough must be rolled out as thinly as possible.
6. Put a full teaspoon of filling on the dough about 1 inch apart.
7. Fold the pastry over and pinch the edges together to seal them.
8. Fry in hot deep fat.
9. Serve hot or cold.

If you do not like to fry them you can cook them in a non-stick pan. In this case you have to add some olive oil in the filling.

FILLINGS
CHEESE

☐ 2-3 cups grated halloumi cheese
☐ 2-3 eggs to mix the cheese
☐ Some dry or fresh mint

MEAT

☐ ½ a kg pork minced meat
☐ 1 medium onion finely chopped
☐ Salt and black pepper
☐ 1 teaspoon cinnamon
☐ A little grated nutmeg
☐ Dry or fresh mint and some chopped parsley
☐ 2-3 tablespoons cooking oil - optional
☐ Some dry wine, optional.

METHOD

1. Place the meat with one or two tablespoons water in a pan and cook on low heat.
2. Add the onion finely chopped.
3. Cook until the meat changes colour.
4. Add the salt, the spices and the herbs.
5. Add the oil and continue cooking.
6. At this stage you can add about half a cup of dry wine.
7. Leave it cooking until the wine evaporates.

RECIPE 23 RAVIOLI FILLED WITH HALLOUMI CHEESE

Ravioli used to be prepared at home and cooked on special days. As it needs a lot of preparation one can order it from some women who specialise in the making of it or buy it frozen. We always make it at home My children used to love helping in turning the pastry machine.

INGREDIENTS
- ❏ 2 cups flour for pastry
- ❏ 1 egg
- ❏ 1 small pinch salt.
- ❏ 6-8 tablespoons warm water.

For the filling
- ❏ Grated halloumi cheese
- ❏ 1 or 2 eggs to mix.
- ❏ A little dry or fresh mint.

METHOD

1. Add the egg to the flour and mix well.
2. Gradually add the water and mix the dough.
3. Work the dough until it becomes elastic.

4. Leave the dough to rest for about an hour.

5. Run the dough through the pastry machine or use a rolling pin until you get it quite thin

6. Place the filling about ½ inch apart.

7. Cover with the other part of the pastry and cut with a small fluted cutter.

8. Cook like pasta in chicken broth and serve with grated halloumi cheese or any other cheese.

You can always multiply the recipe, make more ravioli and freeze them. You cook them frozen. They are very handy to have in the freezer.

CHAPTER 11 - GREEN MONDAY

Green Monday is the first day of lent. In Cyprus, it is a public holiday. On the Sunday before the long fasting period begins, people usually eat and drink with their friends and relations. Because this is the carnival time, we as children, some teenagers and a few grown-ups would dress up on this Sunday and go around visiting neighbours and friends. The children would sing and dance and they would be given money; but these days the celebrations are more artificial and less spontaneous. Now there are organised parties in the big hotels for the children, for which the parents have to pay an entrance fee.

When people wake up on Green Monday, they are ready for more celebrations. Years ago in the villages, young boys organised games and the girls watched. These days, people go out in the countryside with their friends and relations, taking a picnic with them. Some even take tables and chairs. The food is simple, mainly plenty of vegetables, 'greens,' that is why the day is called 'Green Monday.'

On Green Monday, one is not supposed to eat meat, cheese, eggs or even oil. In spite of this the food is appetising. There are olives black and green with crushed coriander and garlic, or green olives in vinegar. Then there are the many kinds of bread, sesame, olive, bread with tahini, spices and sugar, (tahinopitta). There is home-made tahinosalata and taramosalata, or it can be bought from a shop. Pickles of tomatoes, cauliflower, raw artichokes with lemon juice and salt, boiled potatoes and boiled beetroot all add to the feast. And for sweet things, there are jams, marmalades and honeys, including carob honey. Some people eat octopus, squid and cuttle fish, but as a family group, we do not encourage this habit. Instead, on the day before, I make many kinds of bread and a special fruitcake without fat, milk or eggs.

Recipe 24 Tahinosalata

Tahinosalata is an appetising dip; it is always present on a meze table and at the Green Monday lunch.

Ingredients
- [ ] 1 cup Tahini.
- [ ] 2-3 cloves garlic.
- [ ] Some warm water.
- [ ] Lemon juice to taste.
- [ ] Additional water to get the required consistency.

Method
1. Place the tahini in a bowl and beat well until it begins to change to a paler colour.
2. Pour some warm water and beat well; this helps the tahini to swell and somehow to cook. (I understand this is not common practice, I was given this tip by an old lady many years ago.)
3. Start adding the lemon juice and cold water, beating all the time until the required consistency is reached.
4. Crushed cloves of garlic can be added.
5. Decorate with chopped parsley and black olives.

Recipe 25 Taramosalata

Taramosalata is a very appetising dip or salad. It is served as part of a starter on a meze table and during fasting, and always on a Green Monday picnic table.

Ingredients
- [ ] 1 cup taramas, (cod's roe)
- [ ] 1 cup boiled potato, mashed
- [ ] 1 cup white bread, crusts removed, soaked in water and squeezed.
- [ ] 1½ cups olive oil or a mixture of olive oil and cooking oil.

- ❏ 1 cup lemon juice.
- ❏ 1 tablespoon finely chopped onion, (optional)
- ❏ Some black olives for decoration.

METHOD

1. Place the taramas in a piece of muslin and dip it in a bowl of hot water for fifteen minutes to reduce the saltiness.
2. Squeeze it well and place it in a blender.
3. Add the soaked bread, squeezed dry, and the mashed potatoes.
4. Gradually add the lemon juice and olive oil, tasting until you get the flavour you like.
5. If liked, add the finely chopped onion.
6. Serve in an attractive dish and decorate with black olives.

RECIPE 26 CAKE WITH TAHINI –WITHOUT FAT, EGGS OR MILK

INGREDIENTS

- ❏ ½ cup tahini
- ❏ 1/4 cup warm water
- ❏ ½ cup sugar
- ❏ 2 cups plain flour
- ❏ 2 teaspoons baking powder
- ❏ ½ cup orange juice
- ❏ 1-2 tablespoons brandy (optional)
- ❏ 3/4 cup sultanas
- ❏ ½ cup nuts
- ❏ ½ cup –1 cup glacé citrus fruit cut up in small pieces.
- ❏ 1 teaspoon ground cinnamon or to taste

METHOD

1. Beat the tahini with the warm water, add the sugar and continue beating.

2. Fold in the flour, sieved with the baking powder and the cinnamon, alternating with the orange juice and the brandy if used.

3. Add the fruit carefully.

4. Pour into a greased and floured tin, preferably a loaf tin.

5. Bake in a moderate oven at 175°C. for about 45 minutes.

CHAPTER 12 - LENTEN FARE

And the Lord God took the man and put him into the Garden of Eden to dress it and to keep it. (Genesis Chapter 2, verses 15-17).

Man is not supposed to be the king of the Universe to use, or rather abuse it as he likes; he was created to dress it and to care for it. There is a connection between this thought and the Greek Orthodox Church, as I shall now explain:

There are three main fasting periods, which are set out by the Ecumenical Synods.

There are forty days of fasting before Christmas. This is a relatively easy fast as one is allowed to eat fish up to the 12th of December. In August there are fifteen days of fasting. This period starts on the 1st of August and ends on the 15th, the day of the Assumption of the Virgin Mary. This is a pleasant period to fast as there are so many vegetables and fruit around and in the heat of August this lighter food is what one needs.

The longest fasting period is before Easter as it lasts fifty days. This long fasting period is quite complex. Fasting is gradual. On the Sunday of the Apocreo (fasting of meat) one is allowed to eat all kinds of food including plenty of meat, cooked in many ways; souvla usually, young lamb or young goat cooked on an open charcoal fire. After this Sunday, for the following week, one is supposed to abstain from meat and eat fish, cheese and eggs. The next Sunday is the last day before the long fasting begins; It is called the Sunday of Tyrinis, which means the Cheese Eating Sunday. The Monday known as Green Monday is the beginning of the long and more comprehensive fast.

Fasting is not intended to crush the spirit or to undermine the body. So what, then, are its purposes? For spiritual reasons, for health, self-control, self-discipline and for protecting the environment of the animal kingdom: Man is supposed to dress and to keep the garden.

As an example, I would like to mention that sheep and goats have their offspring in late December or early January. Usually fasting starts in the beginning of March and lasts for fiftiy days; so plenty of time is given for growth. On Green Monday, the long fasting period starts and lasts until Easter Day.

The first week is a week of strict fasting. One is not supposed to include even oil in his diet until the Saturday. My mother tells me that her grandmother took fasting so seriously that for three days beginning on Green Monday she ate and drank nothing not even water. This was known as the three-day (trimeri) fasting. On the Wednesday she would go to church and take Holy Communion. I find something beautiful in this story because the old lady who was my great grandmother would take everything she might have eaten during these three days and leave it outside the house of a poor person. In those days, more than eighty years ago, there were many people who did not have enough to eat. On the twenty fifth of March, the day of the Annunciation, people were allowed to eat fish.

On the Monday after Palm Sunday, the Holy Week begins. Fasting is very strict during this week. One is not supposed to include even oil in the diet during this week, except for Thursday lunch. During this week people eat olives with home baked bread, olive bread, halva and they make all kinds of soups with pulses. Even today the majority of people fast during this week. A favourite soup is lentil soup with plenty of vegetables. On Good Friday, it is eaten with a spoonful of vinegar in remembrance of Christ. He was offered vinegar and water when He was dying on the Cross. I remember it served by my grandmother on the 29th of August, the day when Ayios Ioannis decapitation is celebrated. On this day one is not supposed to eat even oil. My grandmother would place a heaped soup plate of dry broad beans in a pan, add plenty of water and cook them on the wood fire. When they were cooked she would add more cold water and boil them until they became like purée. In the mean time, she would add a chopped onion, some garlic and some crushed coriander. In the end, she would mix one or two tablespoons of sieved flour with some vinegar, add it to the food, leave it for a few minutes and bring it off the fire.

Another similar dish but a little more substantial is a dish called broad bean food. After the broad beans were cooked, or rather a little before they were completely cooked, my grandmother would add a big handful of pourgouri. When the dish was finished it was served with lemon juice. Lemons were scarce in August but as I have mentioned in other chapters my grandmother kept lemons in straw. This dish is almost a perfect protein as it is a combination of pulses and cereals.

TSORVAS

(a peasant soup for breakfast).

The village housewife was an expert in using the farm produce in feeding her family. She did not have any other choice. There were no shops in the days I am writing about and very little money. People had to have a filling breakfast before they set off for the fields. My grandmother would place the saucepan with water on the wood fire When the water boiled she would add some chopped vegetables, like celery and cabbage if she had any and then some pourgouri. The quantity depends on the amount of water. When the pourgouri was cooked she would pour plenty of olive oil in a frying pan, she would then add plenty of chopped onion and fry it lightly. She would pour this sauce on the soup. Quite often she would add some double baked pieces of bread. This soup was very filling.

CHAPTER 13 - MEMORIES OF EASTER IN CYPRUS

Easter is the most important religious holiday in the Greek Orthodox Church. The week before Easter is called the Holy Week. It is a strenuous week both physically and spiritually. There are special services in both the mornings and in the evenings. The services are moving, especially the one on Thursday evening when Christ is crucified, and Friday evening when Christ is buried. On Friday morning after the service the young women bring an abundance of flowers and spend almost the whole morning decorating the Sepulchre.

It is a time of strict fasting; one is supposed to have oil only for Thursday lunch. Many people take Holy Communion usually on the Holy Thursday or Holy Saturday morning services.

The housewives are busy cleaning the house thoroughly as it is the beginning of spring and, at the same time, they have to get the place ready for the festive day.

Some fifty or sixty years ago, village housewives would wash and place the wheat outside to dry. This was to prepare it for the mill, where it was usually taken on the donkey. The father or grandfather usually undertook this task; the mill was sometimes in another village. It was normally transported in hand-woven sacks.

When the flour was brought back, it was spread out on a clean sheet to cool, before being stored in an earthenware jug (pithari.) In later years, of course, the housewife could purchase some flour from the mills but this had to be supplemented by the local wheat flour.

Early in the Holy week, the housewife, if she did not have a wood-burning oven in her yard, would make sure she could use her neighbour's oven. On Thursday she would prepare the homemade yeast (prozymi) for the sesame bread to be kneaded on Good Friday.

On Easter Saturday she would make the flaounes, which are uniquely traditional to Cyprus. Flaounes consist of a pastry made with milk, vegetable fat and a very rich filling of special cheese and eggs mixed with mint, sultanas and spices. A small piece of homemade yeast is mixed with the filling to make it rise. These were traditionally home made, but now they can be ordered from a bakery.

All these preparations led to the Saturday night service, which everybody in the village had to attend. When the neighbours were passing by, they would knock loudly on your door to make sure you were awake and getting ready to attend the service. In the old days, the priest would stand in front of the 'Holy Place' and ask if everybody were present before he sang the resurrection hymn, or the 'Good Word,' as it was known. It was a very moving experience, which showed the closeness and friendship of the village.

Outside the church there was always a big fire to celebrate the resurrection of Christ. The young people of the village had been bringing wood, for weeks sometimes, in big lorries. In many villages they would make an effigy of Judas place it on the fire and burn it with a lot of cheers.

Many young people stand outside the church with red-dyed eggs, and one person allows his egg to be tapped by the other person's in a mildly competitive and light hearted game, to see whose egg is strongest He who breaks the other person's egg is expected to have won the broken egg. Perhaps I should point here that there were plenty of eggs around as the mothers kept the eggs they collected from their chicken for Easter.

After the service, people went home to enjoy their egg and lemon soup (avgolemono soup), which was cooked in the chicken broth. The chicken was killed and trussed before. Pieces of the chicken like the drumsticks and the wings were boiled for the broth. The rest of the chicken was left for the following day. The soup was made before the church service. In my home we finished it with the egg and lemon after we came from church. There were plenty of flaounes on the table, as every household rich or poor would make them for Easter. They would tap the red eggs with each other for 'CHRISTOS ANESTI'- (CHRIST IS RISEN).

These days many homes have adopted the Greek soup Mageiritsa that is a much richer soup. In Greece, the 'Tsoureki' is the traditional bread, which has now become part of the Cypriot Easter celebrations

RECIPE 27 FLAOUNES

The special Easter bread of Cyprus.

The basic recipe is always the same. Pastry made with fat, milk, eggs and spices; the raising agent is either the home-made yeast, prozymi, or yeast. The filling is a mixture of a good hard cheese, egg, spices sultanas and mint. The raising agent is again prozymi or yeast. There are some variations; almost every housewife has her own little preferences.

I give you my recipe:

For the pastry:
☐ *One kg pastry flour.*
☐ *Just under one cup shortening.*
☐ *½ teaspoon mastiha.*
☐ *½ teaspoon mehlepi. They are both spices used in bread making.*

- 1 tablespoon sugar
- 1 teaspoon. salt
- 2 eggs.
- About 1½ cups warm milk.
- Prozymi the size of an egg, or two teaspoons yeast. In Cyprus dry yeast is used.

For the filling:
- ½ -1 kg hard cheese plus one halloumi
- 8 to 10 eggs
- ½ teaspoon mastiha
- ½ teaspoon mehlepi .
- One piece of prozymi the size of an egg, or two teaspoons yeast.
- One cup sultanas
- Fresh mint. (If not available, use dried mint.)
- For glazing:
- 2-3 egg yolks
- ½ cup sesame seeds.

METHOD
The filling:
1. Place the grated cheese and the grated halloumi in a good size bowl.
2. Add the spices and stir well to make sure they are well distributed.
3. Break the eggs one at a time in a bowl.
4. Dissolve the prozymi in the eggs, add the mixture to the cheese and mix well.
5. The number of eggs needed depends on how dry the cheese is. So do not add them all at the same time.
6. In case you are using yeast, which is the most probable, add the yeast to about ½ a cup flour, one teaspoon sugar and mix

well with some warm milk. When it starts to bubble add it to the cheese mixture and knead well. If you are using prozymi this has to take place eight to ten hours before it is ready to use. If you are using yeast two to three hours is enough.

The pastry:
1. Place the flour in a bowl with the salt, the sugar and the spices well mixed.
2. Add the shortening and rub it in the flour.
3. Break the eggs and mix with the warm milk. Dissolve the prozymi in this mixture
4. Add the whole to the flour and knead until you get a good dough.
5. If you are using yeast proceed as in recipe 27.
6. Cover and leave for a couple of hours to rise.

The finishing:
1. When both the pastry and the filling have risen well it is time to start shaping the flaounes.
2. Separate the pastry in equal pieces .You can make between eight to ten pieces.
3. Before you start using the filling add the sultanas and the mint and mix carefully.
4. Shape the pastry into round pittes of about 15cm diameter and ½cm thickness.
5. Add the filling and shape either in squares or in triangles. Press the ends well with a fork to bind them together.
6. When you finish shaping all the flaounes, glaze them with egg yolks and sprinkle with plenty of sesame.
7. Heat the oven to about 200°C and cook for about 40 to 45 minutes, until they rise and brown well.

You can always make them smaller.

RECIPE 28 EGG AND LEMON SOUP (AVGOLEMONO SOUP)

INGREDIENTS
- ☐ 4 cups chicken broth.
- ☐ ½ cup rice.
- ☐ The juice of two lemons.
- ☐ Two egg yolks.
- ☐ Salt and pepper.

METHOD
1. Heat the chicken broth
2. Clean and wash the rice
3. When the broth starts to boil add the rice
4. When the rice is almost cooked add the salt and pepper and switch off
5. Place the egg yolks in a good size bowl and beat very well. Add the lemon juice, gradually, stirring all the time.
6. With a soup ladle take some soup from the saucepan and add to the lemon and egg mixture stirring all the time to prevent the curdling of the egg. To avoid this you can add some cold broth to the soup before you start the mixing, to bring the temperature down.
7. Return the egg and lemon mixture to the saucepan with the soup stirring all the time.
8. Heat the soup and serve immediately.

INGREDIENTS

☐ ½ cup warm water.
☐ 2 packets active dried yeast.
☐ 1 ½ cups lukewarm milk.
☐ ½ cup sugar.
☐ 1 teaspoon salt
☐ 2 eggs plus 1 egg yolk for glazing.
☐ ½ cup unsalted butter.
☐ 7 – 7 ½ cups sifted white flour.
☐ Zest of one or two lemons.

You can increase or decrease the amount of butter, sugar and eggs according to your taste.

METHOD

1. Sprinkle the yeast over the half-cup of hand hot water. (Hot water will kill the yeast; cold water will retard the growth of the yeast.) Stir it once and let it stand for about ten minutes.
2. In the meantime, heat the milk; add the sugar and the butter in pieces. Do not overheat the milk, if you do, wait until it cools down.
3. In a large bowl, beat the eggs until mixed, add the milk and the dissolved yeast.
4. Stir in half the flour with the lemon zest and mix well with your hand. Add the remaining flour half a cup at a time, mixing well after each addition. Keep adding the flour until the dough pulls away from the side of the bowl in a ball. It should be soft and slightly sticky.
5. Turn the dough out onto a floured board. Sprinkle the dough and your hands with flour, and knead until it becomes smooth, elastic and forms a ball.

6. *Brush the cleaned bowl with melted butter and place the kneaded dough in it. Cover the bowl with a damp cloth and let it stand in a warm place until it doubles in size.*

7. *Turn the risen dough onto a lightly floured board and knead for a few seconds to knock out the air. Let it rise for five more minutes.*

8. *You can shape it into rolls, but at Easter, you can make the traditional tsoureki. Roll each piece of dough with your palms, stretching it to form a strand of about a 40-45 cm. Then plait the dough; you can use three or four strands, or more, to make your loaf.*

9. *Heat the oven to 200°C. Leave the tsoureki to prove. Before putting it in the oven, glaze it with a yolk of egg that has been mixed with milk or water.*

These cookies are good served in winter with coffee and in summer with a glass of lemonade.

RECIPE 30 COOKIES WITH ALMONDS

INGREDIENTS
- ❑ *150 grams shortening.*
- ❑ *1 cup sugar.*
- ❑ *4 eggs, use two whole eggs and two yolks, (keep the two whites for later)*
- ❑ *3 good teaspoons baking powder.*
- ❑ *As much flour as it takes to make a pliable dough (about 4½ cups)*
- ❑ *2 – 3 tablespoons brandy and rose water mixed.*
- ❑ *The zest of one lemon.*
- ❑ *1 cup blanched almonds cut in pieces.*

METHOD

1. *Sieve the flour and baking powder together. Add the lemon zest.*
2. *Cream the fat and sugar together preferably in a mixer.*
3. *Add the eggs one by one, beating all the time. Leave the two egg whites on a plate.*
4. *Little by little, add the flour, brandy and rosewater.*
5. *Stop the mixer and knead by hand, adding more flour, as much as it takes to make a pliable dough, which does not stick to the palm of your hand.*
6. *Shape the dough into small balls, making a dent in the ball. This will be the top of the cookie, dip this into the egg white, and roll the top of the cookie on the blanched almonds.*
7. *Place on greased baking trays and cook in a preheated moderate oven at 175°C until golden brown.*

This recipe makes about 80 medium size cookies. Store them in an airtight container to keep them fresh.

RECIPE 31 REFRIGERATOR COOKIES

INGREDIENTS

☐ *One cup soft shortening.*
☐ *½ a cup sugar.*
☐ *½ a cup brown sugar.*
☐ *Two eggs.*
☐ *2 3/4 cups sifted flour.*
☐ *½ teaspoon bicarbonate of soda.*
☐ *1 teaspoon salt.*
☐ *1 - 2 teaspoons cinnamon*

METHOD

1. Cream together the shortening and the two kinds of sugar.

2. Add the eggs gradually while still beating.

3. Sift together the flour, the soda, the salt, and the cinnamon and stir into the creamed mixture.

4. Mix thoroughly with your hands. Press and shape into a long mould of about 6 cm in diameter. Wrap in greaseproof paper and chill until stiff. (Several hours or overnight). If you want to speed the process you can place the mould in the freezer for a few hours. With a thin, sharp knife cut in thin slices. Place the slices a little apart on an ungreased baking sheet and bake in a moderate hot oven of 200 °C for about eight - ten minutes.

You can omit the cinnamon and instead stir in one tablespoon grated orange rind. Some people suggest mixing some ground almonds into the dough. I prefer to add half an almond on top of the cookie as I find that the cut up almonds in the dough tend to break it.

CHAPTER 14 - AUGUST AND THE FORTNIGH OF FASTING

August is a beautiful month. In spite of the heat, it is blessed in so many ways. Grapes are at their best, sweet and succulent. There are so many varieties of figs, heaps of watermelons on the road for sale, many kinds of vegetables and many more types of fruit. The 1st of August marks the beginning of fasting. This lasts until the 15th, when the Virgin Mary's Ascension is celebrated and fasting is finished.

Memories of what life used to be like fifty or sixty years ago still linger in my mind. Fasting was taken more seriously then. Many people, especially the women, went to church every evening when a special prayer to the Virgin Mary is made. Fasting was very strict during these two weeks. No meat, fish, milk, cheese or eggs were allowed. On Wednesdays and Fridays many women took no oil on their food.

On the 6th of August, which is devoted to Christ the Saviour, they are allowed to eat fish. The night on the 5th as teenagers, we used to sit outside on the threshing floors to wait until midnight for a shooting star and make a wish, which would come true according to the village legend. I do not need to say that we could not always keep our eyes open until then and perhaps the shooting star never happened.

But I must mention here that even today, many people, especially women, observe this fasting period. As there are plenty of fruits and especially vegetables, fasting is not only easy, but interesting too.

In the Greek Cuisine there are many dishes with the name of 'lathera,' which means 'with oil.' These are vegetable meatless dishes. The housewife can use her imagination and create her own recipes according to the available ingredients. The basic principle is to fry the vegetables, for example, eggplants or ladies fingers lightly first and then add plenty of tomatoes. Chopped onion, garlic and other herbs can be added to taste.

The potato was the most common food used. They cooked it in many ways. Like Potatoes Yiahni, stewed potatoes, which could be called a poor man's meal, as it is a very filling dish and relatively cheap. Another good recipe is potatoes 'antinactes' (potatoes which are tossed,) or coriander potatoes. Small potatoes, the size of a big walnut, are washed; then, peeled or unpeeled, fried in deep fat until nice and crispy. The fat is poured off, then dry red wine to which crushed coriander salt and other spices are added. The potatoes are shaken in the pan several times to ensure a good distribution of the wine and the spices.

The aubergine is one of the most popular vegetables in the Mediterranean. Every country, and I suspect every village and every housewife, has her own way of making the most of it. It is much used in the August fasting period. My favourite method is to use medium size aubergines, wash them, cut them in slices, sprinkle them with salt and leave them for an hour to draw out the bitter juices and make them absorb less oil. Rinse well and squeeze out the moisture and pat them dry with kitchen paper. Fry the slices in shallow hot fat and lay them on kitchen paper to remove as much as possible of the fat. After this they can be used in many ways, be placed in a heat proof dish with slices of tomato and rings of onion; a little oil and some water are added and the dish is cooked in the oven. Another way, the fried slices can be served on their own with lemon or a tomato sauce.

Small tender aubergines with the addition of fried onions, garlic and tomatoes can be either baked in the oven or cooked on top of the cooker to make what is called in Turkish Imam Bayildi (the Imam fainted) because supposedly when the imperial chef first created it for the Sultan of the day, he found it so delicious, he lost consciousness).

In Cypriot villages aubergines were often combined with rice to make a filling dish. The aubergine is cut in cubes, salted, rinsed, dried and sautéed with chopped onion in oil for about ten minutes. Grated tomato is added to the pan and left for a few minutes. Water is added and after the aubergine is almost cooked and the water adjusted rice is added to make a delicious pilau.

Another interesting dish common in August is stuffed squash flowers. During fasting the flowers are stuffed with just rice, onion, herbs, spices, finely chopped tomato, a tablespoon of olive oil and some lemon juice to taste. Mincemeat can be included during a non-fasting period.

The aubergine combined with potatoes, courgettes, and mincemeat, then covered with a béchamel sauce makes an excellent mousaka. In Greece the only vegetable used for mousaka is the aubergine. In earlier years, the early summer aubergines were sometimes cooked with lamb. I would like to mention here that I had this dish in a restaurant in Limassol years ago, and also in America cooked by an Iranian lady. It was delicious on both occasions. These days, more fashionable cooking habits, foreign to this area have been imported.

Lately, people's attitudes have changed. The atmosphere is very different these days. People take their holidays in August. The workers' holidays start a few days before the 15th of August and go on until a week after. Many businesses are closed. People enjoy themselves in many ways. The beaches are full; there is a lot of traffic on the road as people try to meet their displaced relatives and friends. People enjoy themselves in many ways, socialising, eating and drinking is one of them. For some of them fasting is difficult but some especially women still insist to keep the tradition. These days bring poignant memories of another August when the second invasion took place and along with many thousands of other people I lost my village, my family house but most of all my sense of belonging.

CHAPTER 15 - ENGAGEMENTS AND WEDDINGS

Engagements took place all the year round, but mostly during the Christmas holidays and especially after Epiphany day the 6th of January when, according to the village farmers, the waters were baptised. If it looked as if it were to be a good year with plenty of rain then more and more engagements were negotiated. Engagements were arranged between the two families. Usually one or two relations, or sometimes a matchmaker, would mediate. I believe that the young people, especially the boys, had their say. During Easter Sunday, Easter Monday and Tuesday, after the Midday Service, there were always organised games outside the churchyard. The girls would be there in their new clothes to attract the attention of a young boy and the boys would try to excel in the difficult games to impress the girls or the special girl. There were other occasions, like the village weddings, when dancing was arranged during the Christmas holidays. These dances were organised by the young people, usually the girls took the initiative. They would find a kind man or woman who had a dichoro and they would get a violin player and a lute player and borrow some chairs from the neighbourhood. Soon everybody in the village knew and almost everybody would go there. It did not cost them anything. A tray was placed in front of the music players and, after the boys danced, they would throw some money. A relation or friend would often put in some money for the girls. During these dances, girls danced together, while the boys watched and when the boys danced the girls stood aside and watched. The dances were traditional folk dancing. Soon after the Second World War modern dancing was introduced as well. These are about the only chances that couples had to get to know each other (if I can call this knowing each other).

An important factor considered before a match was proposed was the family. In my village they liked, those who could afford it, to marry within the village and when possible within the same extended family. Many couples were third cousins. This caused some hereditary health problems like thalassaemia. Another factor always considered was property. As it was a farming village, land was important to help the couple achieve a reasonable standard of life. Many issues had to be discussed and negotiated between the two sides before the final decision was taken. One should not conclude that all was a cold calculation between the grown ups. As a child I remember a cousin of my mother's who was in such agony to learn the response our next-door neighbour would give to the matchmaker, that he climbed on our maple tree to listen to the answer.

Another important issue was the house. Every couple had to have a house to live in, as there were no places to rent. The husband usually provided the house. After the Second World War things changed and sometimes the girl's family provided the house. As the demands for bigger and better houses became the norm, it tended to become a joint effort of both families.

These negotiations came to an end usually at night. A celebration would follow between the two families, very close relations and the matchmaker. If you happen to walk in the village during one of these nights you would hear the noise of chicken as they picked them from the chicken coop to take them to the celebration. I believe the women who carried the live chicken caused them to make more and more noise and so make their success known. The chickens, of course, were to be eaten at the celebratory meal.

If the girl had reached at least sixteen years old, then a proper engagement with a priest who would bless the rings would be arranged. Quite a big celebration feast would be organised. The two families would decide the extent of relations they would invite. In the village relations are really respected. Fifty or sixty years ago, every family would take a live chicken and some foodstuffs. There were many relations there to help kill and truss the chickens that were boiled in huge galvanised copper pans. A few women would come with their special boards to make the corasisima macaroni, which looks like spaghetti but tastes much better. In those days some more dishes were added usually with foods they had in the house or they produced on the land. After the war things started changing and more elaborate food was cooked. The girl's family would kill one two or more, young goats always according to the number of people invited. The goat meat was cooked in the wood oven outside in the yard.

Before the engagement ceremony, when the priest would bless the rings, the dowry agreement was signed. Usually the priest wrote the agreement in the presence of both sides and read it out to them too. The two sides had agreed about everything during these negotiations, even about the length of the engagement; during the night of the engagement everything is finalised with the help of the village priest. The dowry document was a legal document. In the document they would write whatever they were going to give their children: land, animals, and the amount of money they would give towards the building of the house. If they did not have anything to give they would give their blessings. Later with the new Church Constitution the dowry document was not compulsory.

The engagement usually lasted several years - three, four or sometimes even five. The families had to save enough money to help with the building of the house and to carry out the wedding. In those days money did not come very easily. All these negotiations may sound a little cold blooded to us today; on the contrary, it was village wisdom to avoid if possible any misunderstandings. The village is a close society, everybody is related to each other and a break up of an engagement is more difficult than anywhere else. It was very difficult, if not almost impossible, for a girl to get engaged again if her engagement was broken.

During this long engagement the young couple were not supposed to have any relations or really touch each other. But I remember, as a young child, there was a church wedding with a bride in advanced pregnancy. At the same time a similar tragic incident took place in our village. A beautiful girl while still engaged became pregnant and the mother was cursing her as she thought they lost face in the village. The girl was married off but she died during delivery and the entire village believed that it was the result of the mother's cursing. As a rule the young people in those days had to be very careful.

WEDDINGS

I cannot say when the parents started to save or prepare dowry for their children; I believe that at least the mother began as soon as she had the first daughter. Of course the first priority was the house, which in most cases was simple and basic. It was, as a rule, built with mud bricks and plastered with white mud. Richer people built bigger houses with arches (kamares) and dichoro. All during the time of the engagement mother and daughter would be trying, along with the other jobs to do with the land and the house, to get the dowry ready. Sixty or seventy years ago, all or most household materials had to be hand woven. At one time in my village, the bride used to provide up to six dozen sheets along with all the other household items. On the Saturday before the wedding, which always took place on a Sunday, everything had to be ready to show.

The few weeks before the wedding there were many jobs to be done. The couple's mattress was filled with fleece, which was bought from a village shepherd. This wool had to be washed and dried before Saturday, the day before the wedding. In my village they would take

116

the fleeces a few miles outside the village where there was plenty of running water. Usually young girls would undertake this job with the first bridesmaid as leader. It was an enjoyable outing and on their way back the leader would sit on the donkey, which carried the wool and would hold a cane on which she would hang a colourful piece of material. In the evening there would be a good meal waiting for them. The fleeces were hung out to dry until Saturday.

The weeks before the wedding, they had to wash the wheat, spread it out to dry and send it to the mill to be ground. The last week was really busy. In the days until about 1960, people were invited to the wedding by a gift of two beautifully decorated round loaves of sesame bread. They would invite the priest, the godparents, the violin and the lute player. The rich people, those who produced enough wheat, would invite the whole village with the special bread and send it to their friends in the neighbouring villages.

I must point out here, that when they were inviting single people they sent only one of the special breads. The people who did not produce enough wheat invited only the priest and the close relations with the special breads and they gave an ordinary candle to the rest of the families. The mid- fifties introduced the written invitation in the village weddings with some hesitation. In the same week they had to make the bread for the wedding, which in those days lasted for a full seven days. All the relations were there to help. No family could carry out the wedding without the help of their relations. In turn these relations would be helped when they had their children's wedding.

On Saturday evening the wedding started with the sewing of the couple's wedding mattress. The hand woven material, usually in red and white, would be filled with the lamb's wool to be ready for the final work and celebration. Another finer material would be fitted on top. All this time, songs were sung wishing the couple happiness. In the meantime young women were sewing in each corner of the mattress with red ribbon crosses and one in the middle. Only young unmarried women or women who were married once, but no widows were permitted to sew the mattress. The first bridesmaid would provide the red ribbon, the red thread and the needles. In the middle of the mattress they would place a beautiful piece of material where the relations would throw some money. If the groom was there he would throw some money, as he was the beneficiary. The material with the money was safely placed between the two covers of the mattress. The groom would get the money when he needed it. All this time the singing was going on with the women competing with each other. At this stage a small boy was rolled on the mattress for good luck wishing that the couple's first child were a boy. The best man had to pick up the huge mattress, before others picked it up, holding it on his shoulders and dancing. It was a matter of honour for the best man to get the mattress and not allow the people there to take it from him. I should have mentioned that during all this time the music players were there, playing the traditional music and accompanying the singers. The mattress was placed on the bed and the close relations would start to make the bed. First they made the bed in the ordinary way; those who could afford, with hand woven silk sheets. On top they would place one by one all the beautiful sheets, some hand woven some embroidered, all part of the dowry and later the village women would go round to examine everything and comment about it. Even the poorest girl had to provide some beautiful sheets for making the bed on the Saturday before the wedding. This was their life and this is how they got their enjoyment. When this finished there was music and dancing and late in the evening the music players would have their dinner at the house of the bride's parents.

The weddings, as a rule, took place in October after most of the work on the land was finished. The harvesting and the threshing of the wheat and the barley was finished, the watermelon fields too and the winter potatoes were planted. The weather would have cooled down and it was too early for rains. The whole village took part in the wedding so they needed a lot of space outside the house.

On Sunday morning the relations and the friends were there ready to start the cooking. Before the Second World War the food cooked was very simple. They would cook whatever they produced or whatever they would find in the neighbouring town market. They would boil many chickens from their yard and cook macaroni in the broth. They would cook beetroot, which they sliced and cooked with oil some onion and plenty of water. Another dish they cooked was potatoes yiahni or colocassi. All these dishes were cooked without meat. After the Second World War things changed rapidly as people started to work outside the village and bring more money. Later, I shall describe a contemporary wedding.

In the meantime the bride was getting ready. The young village girls were there to help her get ready. All this time the relations and the friends were singing, praising the girl, and wishing her all the best. All these songs were in rhyme and many of them were developed on the spot. One of the songs, which were sung towards the end, was really moving, 'Call her mother to come and place the girdle round her, to give her the wish and give her away.' Tears filled the eyes of the mother and some of the guests. The song was in rhyme. The mother would come kiss the daughter and

The mother placing the girdle on the danghter

119

place the girdle round her daughter's waist. At the same time she would bring the special pot where dry olive leaves, were burning, move it around her daughter's head make a wish and pass the pot round the guests. The olive leaves had been taken to church on Palm Sunday and left there for forty days to be blessed. This pot is made in silver in beautiful traditional designs, it is called kapnistiri and it is always accompanied by the merreha, which is of the same traditional design, it is used to hold the water for sprinkling guests, either rose water or orange blossom water, on special occasions, for example weddings and other church rituals. The people who could not afford a silver set they would either borrow one or use a bronze one. These days there are fine kapnistiria made by the traditional potteries.

The singing would go on; one of the women there might sing something like, 'Today the sky is shining the day is bright, today the daughter is separated from the mother.' If the mother is not very moved she may answer, 'Today all the happiness is in my heart today I marry off my Maria my matsicoritia' (a beautiful wild winter flower). Another woman can continue with something like, 'Today the sky is shining today the day is bright today the eagle is marrying the dove'.

At the groom's house there was a similar tradition. His parents were there with the best man and his friends to help him get ready. A barber was there to shave him and comb his hair. His friends would ruffle his hair several times to have fun. They would then help him get ready. When the bride was ready and the women there had enough excitement, the bride with the parents their guests and the music players (playing all the time) would walk to the church where the groom with his parents was waiting. When the ceremony was finished they would walk to the couple's house accompanied by the priest and the music players. They would be stopped now and then by women who would come outside their house with their special pots, kapnistiria, to bless the couple and sprinkle them with rose water.

When they reached their house after the religious ceremony the priest would bless them and wish them happiness. Next to the bride sat the bridesmaid and next to the groom the best man. They were there to help and offer something to the guests who came to congratulate the couple. The bridesmaid would offer quince preserved in syrup with a teaspoon to the women and the best man a small glass of brandy with some kind of nuts. As it was usually October, the quince was in season. In the meantime, the music players were playing and the young people were dancing. In front of the music players there was always a plate where money was thrown by the boys who danced or by the relations of the girls. Two boys would dance standing opposite each other to a different music than that of the girls; they danced with their heads up to show their bravery and their youthful vigour. The girls danced to a different music, two girls standing opposite each other showing their modesty their femininity by always looking down. The music and the dancing would go on until well after midnight.

Late on Monday morning there was a festive breakfast. Early in the morning the two mothers would make a lot of dough. Later the best man would come with a pair of boiled pigeons. This has been part of the breakfast for the newly married, as pigeons are supposed to be loving birds. The mothers and the other relations would start to roll the dough into pittes fry them and serve them to the new couple with honey.

Monday evening was very important in all the celebrations. Almost all the people in the village would have attended the wedding. They would take their baskets full of nice food. There would be a roast chicken or roast meat and roast potatoes, some little pies, pourekia, filled with grated halloumi mixed with eggs and some mint and many more goodies. People from the wedding would go round the tables and offer some of the food they had prepared. There were enough tables for everybody. Before the guests sat down to dinner they would congratulate the couple and give money as a present. The dancing would go on for hours. Some time during these festivities the couple would get up to dance. This was the big excitement of the evening. The parents would get up to tack money on both the dancers. The grand parents would follow the godparents and the close relations. The amount of money given depended on how rich the parents were, how many children they had to marry off and of course, on how much they made from their produce that year. Before the war people were very careful with money. As people got more money they gave plenty, sometimes a few thousands. After all, they gave the money to their children to help them start their life. Let us face it, it was a nice way to show off.

On Tuesday there was another eating and drinking party. The close relations and perhaps some people who could not attend on Monday, were there to celebrate with the newly weds. In my village, I do not know if it happened in other villages, two strong men would get a long pole; one end of the pole would be placed on the shoulder of one of the men and the other end on the shoulder of the other man. These two men would go round the village and pick a chicken from the yard of close relations or from the yard of people who would not mind. They would then tie the legs of the chicken and hang them on the pole. When they picked enough chickens and produced enough noise they would take them to be killed, trussed, and cooked for the evening party.

On Wednesday, the newly weds would go round the village with their merreha full with rose water visiting people sprinkling them with rose water and inviting them to their house. The people who had not gone to the wedding on Monday or Tuesday would give them some money. What they gave before the war in those days, was very little, sometimes the equivalent of some cents, or shillings.

On Sunday, a week after the wedding the newly weds would have the very close relations: parents, brothers and sisters, bridesmaids and best men to their house for a meal. The wedding celebrations came to an end. The newly weds had to start planning their life and their work on the land they were given by the two sets of parents

After the Second World War, the people started to make more money by working outside the village. They started to build better houses. On the Sunday of the wedding they would cook better food. They would buy old goats or sheep cut it in big pieces and cook it outside on a wood fire in huge galvanised copper pots. They would fry whole potatoes in similar pots. Everybody was there to share the fun and the food. The wedding continued to be celebrated in the same way for many years. With time things started to change, Sunday and Monday were the most important days of the wedding and soon they stopped celebrating on the rest of the week.

Gradually the food was improved. They still bought several animals (usually old ones), cut them in pieces, place them in baking tins and put in the wood oven, and they would use several ovens in the neighbourhood. When the pieces of meat were sealed, they would transfer them into big galvanised pots and place them in the wood oven, which they had to reheat. In later years food became more sophisticated. The pieces of meat were wrapped in aluminium foil and placed in the big pots from the beginning. Each guest was given a plate with a piece of meat, a good piece of macaroni pastichio, a couple of coupepia (stuffed vine leaves) or meatballs and some tomato and cucumber. Sometimes they would make some pourgouri pilav. In Paphos they make a pilau with ground wheat, which is called ressi. They would employ a cook who would cook the meat. The women would make the coupepia and the pastichio. In my village, the few happy years, before the invasion, when people worked hard on their land and produced enough they would use for a typical wedding about eight hundred kilograms of meat. The entire village and many friends from other villages were there to celebrate with the couple and share in all the excitement.

In the years after the invasion, weddings became a meeting place for the people of my village (and I believe for all the refugees) as they were scattered all over Cyprus. This was their chance to see their relations, their friends and their neighbours. A few years after that terrible shock they started again to celebrate the wedding with the same enthusiasm to have what is known a 'village wedding' with plenty of food music and dancing.

CHAPTER 16 - BIRTHS AND DELIVERIES

In the villages of Cyprus, up until perhaps the nineteen fifties, women gave birth at home. In most villages there was at least one midwife. But in some villages the midwife had to be fetched from a neighbouring village. In such a case things were difficult as the main means of transport was the donkey. In the early thirties in my village, Arghaki, there was no midwife. They had to fetch one. As one can imagine some relatives or neighbours were there to help the midwife and to share the drama. Later, in the middle thirties, my village acquired a very good midwife and later another two. Midwives were respected, given some money and whatever the family produced. Sometimes the mother, if she was a dressmaker, would promise to sew a dress or the grandmother would weave some material.

When the baby was born the midwife after attending to the mother would look after the baby. Before she bathed the baby she would rub her or him with red wine where she had dissolved some salt. The salt is antiseptic and the wine is styptic. One can only admire their wisdom in solving health problems. I suppose they had to, living so far away from any sort of medical care. She would then bath the baby wrap him or her very well so well that you would think that the baby was bandaged very tightly. They would then place the baby in a small kneading trough. I think that the shape of the trough and the fact that it was made of wood gave the baby a sense of security.

For talcum powder they would use the leaves of a shrub myrtle –myrtus communis. After the leaves were dried they would pound them in a mortar until they became like powder, they would then add a drop of olive oil and mix it well together. It was then transferred to a little bag made of an old sheet to be used on the baby's buttocks and the baby's skin creases to prevent a rash.

The midwife would visit the mother daily for the necessary treatments. The priest of the village would be invited to go and give a blessing to the people and the house. He would say some prayers, place the cross in the water provided for the purpose and he would go round all the rooms sprinkling the blessed water and giving the cross to be kissed by everybody present except the mother who was allowed only after forty days to enter the church or kiss an icon.

While the mother was lying–in, she was looked after very well. She was not allowed to get up; everything was done for her. What was very important, and at the same time very moving, is the way she was fed by the relations and friends They would agree among themselves who would take food to her each day, as it was customary for each relative or friend to take some food to her once during her lying- in. The food was chicken, pigeons or rabbit as there was meat only on Sunday and not always then. She in return would place double baked sesame bread, koumoulla, on the plates so as not to return them empty. She and her mother would prepare these before her confinement.

A week after confinement, the midwife would come to help her get out of bed and go round all the rooms in the house making the sign of the cross with a sharp instrument on the door of every room or on a piece of furniture. To make these crosses more prominent they would scrape some soot from the pans and add some oil. This suspension of the soot and the oil was used to mark the crosses and make them more obvious.

When the baby was one week old he was taken to church by one of the relations. The priest received the baby at the entrance of the church, said his prayers, took the baby inside the church and if he was a boy he took him to kiss the icons. Forty days after confinement the mother would take the baby to church where the priest would bless both of them and the mother would be allowed to go to church and to take Holy Communion.

CHAPTER 17 - BAPTISMS AND CHRISTENIGNS

Go ye therefore, and teach all nations, baptizing them in the name of the Father and of the Son, and of the Holy Ghost.   St Mathew, chapter 28, verses 19 and 20.

These are the words of Jesus on the day of his Ascension.

Before this, St John the Baptist, son of Zacharias, was in the wilderness, preaching the baptism of repentance for the remission of sins (St Luke chapter 3 verses 2 and 3). The baptism that John urged the people of his time to take was a symbolic baptism; he did not have the right to forgive sins.

Following Jesus' example his disciples started to baptise people. The sins they had committed up to that time were believed to be forgiven. These days in the Orthodox Church, baptism is performed at a very young age, usually before the children are one year old. In this case it is believed that the Original Sin is erased.

Baptism is always a time of feasts and celebration. The first baby is baptised by the first best man and the second by the first bridesmaid. The name of the baby is quite often a time of disagreement between the two families and sometimes among the couple. Usually the chosen name is the name of the paternal grandfather for a boy; if one of the grandparents is dead usually they choose his or her name. Quite often a saint's name is given to the baby either because the baby was born on the saint's name day or because the mother prayed to this special saint for help during pregnancy and delivery.

127

The godfather buys the necessary clothes for the baby and always a gold cross with a long chain. He also provides a towel and a bar of soap for the priest to wash and dry his hands over the baptismal font, when the ceremony is finished.

Baptism is one of the seven sacraments, the one that entitles the baby to enter Jesus' Church. The other six are the Chrisma, Holy Communion, Penance, Holy Order, Matrimony and Holy Unction. A sacrament is defined as a religious rite regarded as a channel to and from God, a sign of grace.

The first part is the catechism; this is why the godfather has to be an Orthodox. The priest reads the set prayers and asks that through the grace of Jesus everything evil gets out of the baby. At this point the priest asks the godfather who is all this time holding the baby (who is most of the times screaming) to renounce the devil and identify with Christ. The renunciation is done not only with words but with gestures too, by making a dismissive sound with the mouth. At this point the godfather recites or reads the Creed, a proof of his identification with Christ.

The baby is undressed and the priest rubs the baby with the oil which he has already blessed. The oil is taken to church by the godfather. A little oil is poured in the baptismal font by the priest, as always in the sign of the cross. This is symbolic like the athletes in Ancient Greece were smeared with oil before entering the stadium. The baby is entering his own spiritual struggle. The baby is immersed by the priest in the baptismal font in the name of the Father and of the Son and the Holy Ghost. Three times the baby is immersed and withdrawn from the water. This triple immersion and withdrawal symbolises the burial and resurrection of Christ. The priest lifts the baby out of the font and places it in the arms of the godfather who is holding open a rather large piece of white material called the Myropanni, which means the Holy Myron cloth or the chrism cloth.

I believe that what follows is perhaps the most important part of the ceremony. The priest anoints the baby with the Holy Myron, the Chrism, which I shall explain in a moment. He anoints the forehead, the back, the palms, the soles, the stomach; making each time the sign of the cross, with a little brush that he dips in the bottle of the precious oil. Finally, he cuts four small pieces of hair, making the sign of the cross, from the baby's head. The priest is saying: 'The hair of the servant of God is cut in the name of the Father and of the Son and of the Holy Ghost'. This is the second Sacrament, the first being the baptism that is the admission of the child into the Church. The Holy Myron is a mixture of 57 aromatic oils; they are blessed in church in prayers and in the mass, beginning on Palm Sunday and finishing on the Thursday before Easter. This takes place in the Patriarchal Church in Constantinople. A high Prelate, who brings the Holy Myron to his Church, represents each Church. The aromatic oils symbolise the different charisma, of the Holy Ghost: Love, Peace, Happiness, Faith, Wisdom, Temperance, and many more.

This ceremony is called the Chrisma. I must point out that all the Orthodox Churches, like the Church of Russia, Albania, Bulgaria and the rest take the Holy Myron from Constantinople. All the churches contribute either in aromatic oil, like the church of Bulgaria which sends the rose oil, or in money to help buy the aromatic oils. This participation creates a sense of the unity of the far-flung and multi-ethnic Orthodox Churches and the product, the Chrism Oil, is therefore especially powerful.

The baby is given Holy Communion after this. The godfather, holding the baby in his arms, is ready to walk home with the priest singing. 'All those who are baptised in Christ are armoured in the spirit of Christ'. The godfather, with the baby, the priest, the boys with the cross and the candles, accompanied by the relations and the friends walk home to the mother. The priest gives the baby to the mother at the same time telling her; 'Take your baby, baptised, anointed with the Chrisma, and enlightened by the Holy Ghost'. He advises her to look after the baby well up to the age of seven. The mother in her turn bends down kisses the hand of the priest and she receives the baby.

After the service a meal follows with the priest, the church singers, the godparents, the grandparents, the brothers and sisters and the close relations. At the time I am writing about, the food was simple but wholesome, they cooked mainly what they produced. They killed and cooked chicken. The old chicken they boiled and they cooked macaroni in the broth; it was served with plenty of grated halloumi.

They cooked the younger chicken in a yiahni with potatoes, or with colocassi. In the summer they might have green beans. Some families would have killed a young goat from their yard and some others might buy some meat. Fifty or sixty years ago all the food was as a rule cooked on top of the fire. The men were served first, the women looked after them. After the men finished the women had their turn.

The baby was not bathed for three days; as a matter of fact the baby had to stay in the same vest and the top blouse up to the third day when the godfather came to bath him and to wash the clothes. The Myropanni is washed with the baby's clothes. This happened usually in the evening and a good supper followed.

The parents had a great respect for the godparents; they would get up when they entered the room and often they would kiss their hand. They kept a close relationship and they supported each other in village problems.

Sometimes the Christening took place in monasteries or in churches outside villages. Many years ago the reason was mainly religious. The parents would promise in their prayer to have the baby baptised in the certain church. I would like to mention here that my mother who was born on May 1908 was baptised in the church of

Panayia Trooditissa on the Troodos Mountains. We have been lucky to have a page from the monastery noting that she was baptised on the 14th of August of the same year, the day before Virgin Mary's Ascension. On this day there is always a fair on the said monastery. It is difficult to imagine the preparation and the difficulties they faced travelling by donkey from the Morphou area to the monastery with a baby. I imagine they had to carry not only food for them but for the animals too. I should point out that my grandmother lost a couple of babies before she had my mother who was named Styliani after Ayios Stylianos who is the protector of babies; he is painted always with a baby in his arms. I understand from my mother who went several times to Kykko Monastery on the mules that they would start in the evening after supper and arrive there at dawn.

What they really needed were strong, tame animals 'saddled' with very soft thick coverings so that the riders could lie forwards on their mules and take a nap when possible on the journey.

After the Second World War, things started changing. People made more money and so they spent more. They started using the wood oven outside in the yard to make kleftico. They enriched the meal with stuffed vine leaves or meatballs or both and later with macaroni pastichio.

As the village acquired a few buses many people chose to have the christenings in monasteries or in churches out in the countryside. They would hire a bus, it was paid for by the parents and probably the godparents, relations and friends were invited to join the party. They used to take food with them and have it cooked at the restaurant near the church. This was a chance for them to visit the church of the chosen saint and most important, they had a day away from the village and the daily rounds. In 1964 my youngest daughter was baptised in a very old and beautiful church Acheropeitou, on the Kyrenia beach near the village of Lapithos. The four-month old baby charmed everybody as she enjoyed the whole ceremony and was full of smiles all the time. After the ceremony we went to a restaurant where the tender veal we took with us was made into a tasty Souvla. As a first course we cooked the macaronia trypita (with a hole) made by my mother the day before. Another advantage was the fact that the numbers of guests could be limited to a manageable number.

Some years after the1974 invasion, when things became a little more normal people started celebrating christenings in a bigger way, inviting more people. Even so, they always decide up to what degree of relationship they have to invite to avoid misunderstandings. The main reason, I think, is the fact that they could all get together, travel from the different parts of the island where they made their temporary home and spend some time with relations and friends. I cannot help thinking that somehow they are hoping that their unmarried daughters and sons will meet a suitable boy or girl from the village.

After the christening there is always a lunch cooked and served by the restaurant at a price agreed before. It is left to the godparents whether they are to contribute towards the cost of the meal; usually they do. It is worth mentioning that the guests give money as a present and so the cost is largely covered.

CHAPTER 18 - FUNERALS

The whole village got together whether it was something festive like a wedding or something sad like a funeral. Everybody knew when someone in the village was dying. They would visit, take something suitable for him to eat, and ask for forgiveness and forgive at the same time.

During the last stages of the patient's illness the priest would be called to offer him Holy Communion. As a child, I remember the priest reading in dim light to the dying the Holy Unction before he offered Holy Communion. We as children were present everywhere; everything that happened in the village was part of our life. Our parents did not try to protect us from contact with death. We attended all the funerals and walked with everybody else to the cemetery which was a few kilometres outside the village. I must point out here that the people who were working on the fields would leave their work and attend the funeral.

We were not scared of the dead; death was a continuation of life. The death of Nicos Koustrouppos did not scare us, but it did shock us He had climbed up a tree to pick a few green almonds, by the well, but he lost his grip and fell in. Some people who were working ran to save him but they were too late. He was only six years old. We had attended the same class; he was a handsome and delightful boy, always neat and tidy. We missed him so much in the class.

If someone died in the afternoon, he would be buried the following day. The close relations, friends and his neighbours would keep him company all night. In earlier years, the priest and any other educated men would read the Psalms of David (151 Psalms in all). These days everything is more formal and impersonal. They take them to a Chapel of Rest. The dead person is dressed with great respect by someone in the village who knows how to do it. This has to be done before the body becomes too cold and difficult to manage. They take three pics (the equivalent of two yards) of unwashed calico, called the misaro. They open a small hole at the top by burning it with a candle; they enlarge the hole by tearing it in the four directions to make the sign of the cross. They robe the dead person by passing this over his head. They then dress him in his best clothes and shoes.

Before the funeral, the church bell would be rung in a particular continuous rhythm which everyone understood and people would leave their work on the fields and come to the funeral.

When I was a child, the dead were not placed in a coffin. They were taken to the cemetery on a wooden bed (xilocrevato) which was the property of the church. It was just a piece of strong board with two handles on each side. The dead were covered with a sheet and buried just as they were. Buried in this simple manner the corpse decomposes more quickly.

In older days quite often an old person, who was given something for charity, would come out with the wish, 'May the grave of your, naming the person, becomes fragrant', meaning that the flesh disappears from the bones quickly. On the other hand if someone wanted to make a terrible curse he would say, 'I wish and pray to God that his body will not decompose'. These two wishes express the folk belief that in order for the soul to reach God the flesh has to dissolve leaving the bones relatively clean.

When a priest died, he was taken to church, and he was seated on a chair with a bible in his hands. All of us had to bend and kiss the bible and his right hand. He was buried sitting on a chair. The late Archbishop Makarios put an end to it. He had the subject discussed at the Holy Synod and a decision was taken on the matter.

During the funeral there was always a lot of crying and lamentation by women; men were usually silent. Even at the funeral of an old person, the crying and the lamentation could not be avoided. When my paternal grandfather, the priest, died in 1942 one of his daughters showed her grief by composing sad rhymes, which she sang in a wailing voice during the last part of the service and during the walk to the cemetery. One of the other daughters just fainted. The daughters felt that they had to grieve their parent.

A lovely old lady, mother of the late Yiannis Pipis, asked her son to accompany her to the grave with music. He was a good violinist. He played the violin, all the way to the cemetery. Perhaps he was creating the piece then and there. It was a change we the children loved it; Thinking back I do not think that the grief or the respect were less real. They were real and more moving too. But nowadays in the towns educated women are uncomfortable with public lamentation and they try to grieve more quietly.

During the years before the World War and a few years afterwards, I do not remember young people dying of fatal illnesses, but quite a number died in accidents. The weeping and the lamentation at the funeral of these people was something unbelievable. Odysseas Konomou was found drowned in his borehole. Some years later Tooulos Kneknas fell in the borehole he had just finished, and as he was telling his relations and friends who were celebrating with him to be careful. These are a few examples which left their mark on everybody in the village.

Because it is very difficult to carry a heavy corpse for several miles in the heat of the day, village custom required that after a man had walked a couple of hundred yards, another man would come up to his side from the procession and take over the burden for him. In this way, many men participated personally in the task of managing the movement of the dead person from the house to the church to the cemetery.

One woman with a plate with olive oil and another one with an earthenware jug full of water are walking in the front of the funeral. In many villages they take a plate of kolliva too. The dead are placed in the grave by four strong people who use a rope to make the job easier.

The priest while praying for the dead pours the oil in the grave in the sign of the cross and he breaks the plate .The men start to throw the soil back to the grave. Each of the friends and the relations throw three small handfuls of soil and bid the dead farewell saying at the same time "may God rest your soul in peace". The water in the jug is poured on the grave; some of the people wash their hands after throwing the soil to the grave. The kolliva is thrown on the grave while the jug and the plates are broken onto the grave.

Outside the cemetery there are trays of small pieces of bread with a bowl of olives, pieces of halloumi and some wine, usually sweet wine. This is given for consolation. Everybody is expected to have a small piece.

The women wear black for a long time; the length of time differs according to the closeness of the relation to the deceased. The men wear black shirts and they grow a beard.

Some time after the funeral the family would put up a wooden cross on the grave. In the late fifties they started to have crosses made of marble and to build the grave in marble.

CHAPTER 19 - THE SATURDAYS OF THE SOULS (PSYCHOSAVVATO)

In the Greek Orthodox Church, and I believe in the Catholic church as well, some time is devoted to the dead. In the Catholic Church, it is celebrated on the 1st of November. In the Greek Orthodox Church the days of the Souls are not fixed on the same date, as they are set according to Easter. They are always on a Saturday.

The first Saturday devoted to the Souls is the Saturday before the Sunday of the Apocreo. (this is the Sunday, a week before lent begins, the last day people are supposed to eat meat, until Easter.) On this Sunday the Bible on Judgement is read in the Sunday Service.

"When the Son of man shall come in his glory, and all the holy angels with him, then shall he sit upon the throne of his glory" .St Mathew chapter 25th verse 31 ~ 46. So on the Saturday before the Sunday of the Judgement the people think of their dead ones. On the Friday evening they take kolliva {boiled wheat mixed with sesame and decorated with blanched almonds raisins and pomegranate seeds when available} and a specially baked loaf of bread, decorated with the cross or some church symbols. They take the list of their dead ones, starting from grandparents or even great grandparents. The priest takes the list and he says a special prayer for the dead.

The other Saturday devoted to the souls is the Saturday before the Pentecost. On the Sunday of the Pentecost after the Service there are three kneelings with special prayers. The last kneeling is devoted to the dead.

I remember the Saturdays of the Souls; as a child they had a special meaning to me My mother would prepare a plate of kolliva and bake a special loaf of bread and send me on the Friday Evening, with the special list to the church, as she was always busy, where I met more girls with the same mission.

What I still remember vividly is that both my mother and my grandmother would not sew or even hold a needle on the Saturday of the Souls as they might hurt the dead soul. They would never do the washing on the Saturday of the Souls as they did not want to throw dirty water. They even avoided having a bath on that day.

This reminds me of a beautiful poem by Mavillis, I shall try to give a translation although, I know it is a poor one:

OBLIVION

Lucky are the dead who forget

The grief of life. When the sun sets

And the dusk follows, don't weep for them,

Whatever your pain.

At this hour the souls are thirsty and go

To the crystal spring of oblivion

The water will be filled with mire

If the people shed a tear for them they love,

If they drink clouded water, they remember again,

Crossing fields of asphodiles,

Old sorrows, sleeping in their thoughts.

If you cannot help but cry in the afternoon

Let your eyes lament for the living

They want but they cannot forget.

CHAPTER 20 - KEEPING THE CELLAR FULL

In the years before the Second World War, the farmer had money only a few times a year. With this money he had to pay many of his own commitments. The wife was not given housekeeping money, at least not on a regular basis. She had to store food in many ways.

In the Cyprus village traditional cooking there was a lot of preserved food. Farmers had to rely on what they produced or what they would be given in exchange for work they did for other villagers. Wheat was the staple food. Bread was made every week. And additionally in the summertime, they prepared enough pourgouri to last them the whole year. They made trahanas, a mixture of sour milk or yoghurt mixed and cooked with cracked wheat, shaped in small pieces, dried in the sun and used for soups during the winter months. They made their noodles, dried and kept them for winter. But most importantly they had flour to make some dough and cook something good when they came in late from the fields.

Another food the village mothers kept for a whole season was pulses. They tried to preserve the different kinds as soon as they picked them. Black-eyed beans were put in the oven after the bread had been taken out or they put them in a bag or basket, dipped them in boiling water and dried them. These days I buy my pulses from the farmer, I place them in the freezer for two or three days, then take them out to dry completely in the sun. The housewives also cracked broad beans early in the summer then placed them out to air and then in bags or in containers adding one or two pieces of garlic to ensure that they were kept unspoiled. Olives both black and green were preserved in many ways.

Many farmers reared a pig, which they killed around Christmas. All the relations, neighbours and friends were invited to a party with lovely food. The main dish was afelia, which is pork cooked in red wine with cumin and crushed coriander seeds. Another dish was the cooked belly pork, which was boiled with beetroot, some onion rings and some sliced cabbage if available.

The best dish was the ofto, which was cooked in the ashes of the wood fire that had been lit to boil water for cleaning the pig. The liver and pieces of meat from the pig were wrapped in old calico, which was made wet so that it wouldn't burn. Salt, pepper and spices, like cumin and crushed coriander, were added before cooking.

The meat was preserved in several ways. They rendered the lard for use in cooking. The loin was marinated in wine, salt, coriander, cumin and other spices for a few days. The meat was cut into many small pieces and was marinated together with the loin. The loins were placed outside in the sun to dry and be made into lountza. The pieces of meat were placed in the intestines and hung in the sun to dry. These are the sausages. In every district different spices were added, but the basic recipe was the same. In the mountain villages they smoked their sausages.

They enjoyed both the lountza and the sausages for a few days. Thinking always of the days ahead of them they fried the sausages and lountza in the lard they had rendered and then placed them in special earthenware containers with the lard. This kept for months and they took some out for the family and the farm workers. Quite often they kept them until the harvest of barley and wheat. When they chose the meat for the lountza and the sausages they left behind the head and some pieces of meat. Three or four days after the killing of the pig they boiled the head and the meat, they had another party only - smaller, and they made brawn. It was made without gelatine. Instead the juice of seville oranges was used. It was delicious.

It was a constant responsibility and worry for the mother what she would place in the pan every evening. Before leaving for the fields every morning, she would leave some bread and olives in a basket and possibly some halloumi cheese for the children when they came home for lunch. One of the best foods she made and stored for months in whey was halloumi cheese. To achieve this, she had a lot of work and planning. First she had to acquire the goats. She would start with one or two goats and gradually she would have more goats usually by keeping some of the new-borns. She would milk the goats in the evening, pour the milk into a clean jar, which was put in a basket or a bucket then hung from the ceiling to keep cool and clean. In the morning she would milk the goats again. It was impossible to make the cheese with the small amount of milk she had daily from her goats. So a number of neighbours, friends or relations (between ten to fifteen women) would decide to join forces. To make the effort worthwhile they had to have between thirty five to forty litres of milk to make the cheese. By joining forces they could do it easily. Each member of the group in turn would be given the milk for four or five days. Every woman had a book recording the names of the members and the days she was to receive milk. Early in the morning, the whole village was awake with the women exchanging news and gossiping while taking the milk to the particular group member. The cheese maker would receive the milk, pour it in the big pan and credit the woman with the amount of milk she delivered. She would record the amount of milk in okes and in cups. By the end of the four or five days, when her time for cheese making was up everybody in the group knew with how much milk she was credited or debited. In the village there were many groups cooperating in this way. I cannot help thinking that this is the beginning of the Cooperative ideal.'

CHAPTER 21 - WHEAT, OUR DAILY BREAD

About ten thousand years ago, ancient man was a hunter-gatherer. The tribes were constantly on the move, searching for food, hunting animals, fishing and picking fruits. When it was discovered that certain types of wild grasses, cereals, could be cultivated and used for food, tribes gradually settled in one place to grow their crops and rear their animals.

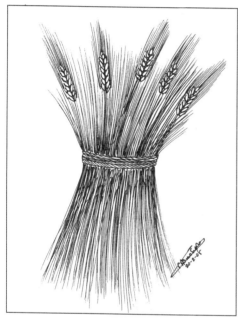

A sheaf of wheat

In most countries, cereals are the staple food for the majority of the population, because they are relatively cheap compared with meat and other foods. Even in wealthy countries, cereals are still eaten in large amounts. Nutritionists stress that most of the calories in a healthy diet should be from whole grains.

In Cyprus, wheat was not only a staple food it also played an important part in every phase of social and religious life. Memorial services for the dear departed are held; forty days, three months, six months, nine months and twelve months after death, and then yearly

143

for many years. When people hold a memorial service for their loved ones, or celebrate in church a special religious holiday, they prepare 'kolliva.' This is boiled wheat, enriched with sesame seeds and decorated with blanched almonds, sultanas or raisins. Pomegranate seeds are also used when available. The kolliva is usually served on a straw tray, (paneri), but these days if no paneri is available the kolliva is served on ordinary trays. Either way, this ritual food is arranged attractively with coloured designs, usually crosses.

For both the memorial services and for the celebration of Saint's days, one small tray is taken to church in the evening and one larger, early on the morning of the service. The kolliva is offered to the congregation after the service. It is a very tasty and nutritional food. Wheat served with almonds is almost a perfect blend of protein. It can be eaten for breakfast as a cereal, with milk. Children love to get a handful of kolliva and eat it on its own. I remember visiting the teachers training college when I was a young girl. It was in Morphou, and the Principal was an enlightened Englishman. I saw that their breakfast consisted of kolliva with milk and sugar. When kolliva is taken to church it is always accompanied by a number of special loaves of bread, 'arti'. This word, meaning 'bread,' is only used for church bread. It is this word that is used in the phrase from the Greek version of the Lord's Prayer; "Our Father, who art in heaven, give us this day our **daily bread**", «Τόν ἄρτον ἡμῶν τόν ἐπιούσιον».

This church bread is not kneaded with ordinary bread dough because it should be of a different consistency. The arti are stamped with a special stamp, which was usually purchased in Jerusalem when people visited the Holy Land. Good households possessed one of these stamps, and those that did not, could always borrow. People usually took five or six ordinary sized arti, and a larger one called a pentarti, (five arti). This larger artos was stamped in five places, once in the middle and four times around it.

Thirty or forty years ago, arti were baked at home. Now

everything is ordered from a bakery. Quite often, a sesame bread, which is larger, is taken to church along with the other loaves. Pieces of it are handed out along with the Kolliva as the congregation leaves the church. After the long service, I find both the Kolliva and this special bread delicious.

You may be wondering what happens to all this bread. Well, the priest blesses some and it is served in small pieces to those in the congregation who have not eaten anything before the service. The rest of the arti is the property of the priest, who often shares it with those who help him in church and he might give it to poor families in the village.

The celebration of some Saints' days is joyful; usually these celebrations are taken over by the children of the family when the parents die or become too old to deal with it. After church, a big lunch used to follow to which the priests, the singers in the church, and all the people, rich or poor, were invited. The women, usually relations or friends, who came to help, used to have their lunch after they made sure that the men had finished theirs and left. During lunch, the priest would always sing a beautiful hymn, praying for the family. My parents used to celebrate the Pentecost, fifty days after Easter. It still brings back beautiful memories. At one point during this service the priest and congregation had to kneel three times and my mother had to provide the cushions for the priest. After the service, a big row of tables was set outside on the arched veranda and a splendid lunch of a variety of dishes was served. I loved it; the house was full of people all day.

In those days, wheat was the most important food item produced on the plains of Messaoria and Morphou. A man's wealth was measured in how many Kilos of wheat he produced. When we speak of *Kilos* in this connection, we do not mean the metric weight used today. The *Kilo* was a cylindrical container containing between twenty-five and twenty-eight metric kilos according to the wheat quality.

The wheat harvest was in May. It was a very busy time for these villages as everything was done by hand. Since no machinery was used, workers were very much in demand, and they came from other villages such as Pyrgos. As the workers had a wide choice of employers, they chose to work for those who provided the best meals. They started work very early in the morning so they needed good, substantial meals. For breakfast, a good housewife would make a big saucepan of pourgouri pilau, which would be topped with home made sausages, fried eggs and lountza, (pieces of pork preserved in lard). Lountza was kept from the winter when the pig was killed. For lunch, they often had boiled potatoes, boiled eggs, boiled beetroot, olives and plenty of the traditional Cyprus vinaigrette (a bottle of olive oil and vinegar shaken together before use) to make the salad. With this

A couple mowing

146

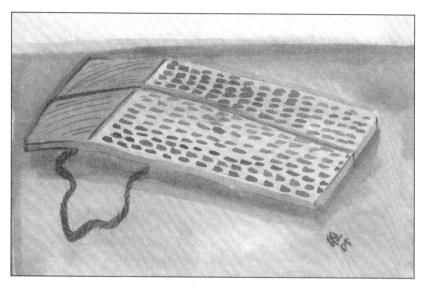

The dukani.

Threshing

147

they drank plenty of wine. They sat on the ground to eat their meals, which had been cooked over a wood fire, at home in the morning. Then for dinner, pulses with vegetables, fried halloumi and fried potatoes. On the last night, they would invariably have fried pastries (pittes) as well.

The life of the village housewife was really very difficult. The men harvested the wheat and the women followed behind them tying it in bundles, which were then transported on donkeys to the threshing floor. Here the bundles were piled in heaps until threshing time came. In the late afternoons we would sit around the threshing floor with wheat bundles scattered all round us. We would cut away the stems of some of the wheat, which we saved to make straw trays and baskets. Today, everything is done by machine so this opportunity no longer exists.

The threshing took from two to three weeks according to the size of the harvest. Wheat bundles would be spread on the threshing floors and the oxen would go round and round the wheat bundles all day, with a short break at lunchtime. They drew a wooden board called a dukani, studded with sharp-edged pieces of granite until the wheat bundles were broken down. More bundles were added until the heap of wheat bundles was finished. Then the oxen continued until all the wheat grain was released.

At this stage it was called 'malama', which means 'gemstone', as it was shiny like a precious stone and valuable at the same time. The malama, a mixture of wheat and straw, was piled up, and then a group of men would begin 'winnowing' the mixture, a process that separated the wheat from the chaff. They used special teethed wooden shovels to throw the malama in the air. The grain, being heavier than the chaff, would fall to the bottom of the heap. When necessary, it was sieved by the women who followed them.

The wheat was piled and checked by inspectors and marked. One tenth of it was paid to the government in tax, a system continued by the British Government until about 1930. The remaining wheat was then stored in a special room such as an attic, where it could be kept dry, away from humidity.

The wheat was mainly used for bread making in the villages. Years ago there were no bakeries in the countryside. Every family had to bake their own bread, usually on a Saturday. If by chance they ran out of bread, they would borrow a loaf from a neighbour.

The wheat was washed, dried, and taken to the mill to be ground. When the flour was brought home, it was placed on a big sheet to cool down before being put in an earthenware vessel, (pithari). For bread making, a home-made yeast called 'prozymi' was used.

A good housewife wouldn't limit herself to simple bread. According to the time of year, she could make olive breads, halloumopittes or titsiropittes. Olive bread was enriched with olives, chopped onions, mint and fresh coriander. Halloumopittes was enriched with pieces of halloumi cheese and fresh or dried mint. Titsiropittes was bread dough with the addition of pieces of lard after rendering lard for fat. These freshly baked breads would be served with eggs and potatoes baked whole on the hot ashes of the oven, plenty of olive oil and whatever vegetables they had. It was customary to give some 'warm bread' as they called it to the neighbours or to passers by. If nobody happened to be around, my grandmother would leave a small piece of warm bread on top of the oven. Bread making day was hard work for the housewife. She had to make sure she had gathered enough wood to heat the oven and the water. If she had a good husband, this was taken for granted, but a number of women in the village had to struggle for everything. But it was always a happy day for the children, as mother would present them with some of the fresh baking.

My grandmother, when she came home tired from the fields,

would either have left some pulses soaking to be cooked for dinner, or she would make a handful of dough. This was made with just flour, water and salt. The dough was rolled out into a big round sheet; sprinkled with flour to prevent it from sticking then rolled around the rolling pin. This could make several dishes, such as toumatsia, a kind of home-made pasta: strips were cut off the dough sheet, something like lasagne, and the strips were then cut into yet smaller pieces. The toumatsia were put onto a paneri (straw tray,) the flour was shaken off the strips of dough and they were cooked in boiling water. As each strip was taken from the water, it was sprinkled with lots of grated halloumi or dry anari. Was it, perhaps, the quality of the flour, or the home made cheese, or the fact that food was not so plentiful that made it so delicious? It seems a shame that nobody makes this nowadays.

Many years ago, people made their own macaroni at home. They used flour, water and a little salt; several different kinds were made in my home village near Morphou.

Macaroni Trypita, (macaroni with a hole.) A handful of prepared dough was taken and rolled around a special straw from a wild shrub. By rolling it with their palms on a floured board, they would make the macaroni about one and a half inches long, and this was placed on a paneri. The macaroni was boiled in chicken broth. An older chicken from the yard would be killed, boiled, and the broth used for the pasta stock.

Macaroni Korassissima (girlish macaroni) was very thin, like spaghetti, without a hole. (I leave it to your imagination why macaroni without a hole was called girlish). After the dough was prepared, it was rolled by both palms on a smooth board and placed on a paneri in a spiral form. It was customary to make this kind of macaroni for an engagement party. Several women would sit around the big room with their special boards making the macaroni. These would be boiled in chicken broth, as all the relations and friends who were invited would come with a live chicken, which was killed and trussed there.

150

Fithes Noodles was made with plain dough, just flour and water. In the summer evenings, the women would gather outside to make enough noodles to last them all winter. They would sit outside a woman's house; she would provide the straw trays on which the noodles were placed as they were hand rolled. Fithes was left to dry thoroughly and stored in special calico bags, usually made from old sheets. The following evening, another woman would invite the neighbours to help her. These evenings went on until they had enough noodles to last the winter. As a child I used to love these evenings, as I said earlier, there were no cars in those days. It was a hard life, but it had a lot of compensations, such as neighbourliness and a sense of belonging. Noodles were used just like pasta is today, or as a complement to pourgouri pilau or made into a pilau. I still make noodles; I roll them by hand when I sit down to watch TV. I find the process very relaxing.

To make Pourgouri, after the wheat is cleaned of foreign matter and washed very well, it is placed in a large saucepan and covered with cold water. The pan is put to heat on the fire. As the water evaporates, more cold water is added until the wheat begins to swell. At this point, it is poured into a basket to drain, and sprinkled with cold water to stop it from cooking. When it has drained completely, it is put on mats to dry. This takes between three and five days depending on the weather. Before the invasion, my mother used to grind pourgouri at home with a big stone mill. Nowadays, we take it to the mill at Yiolou village to be ground. When we bring it home, it has to be winnowed to remove the husks.

RECIPE 32 HOW TO PREPARE KOLLIVA

1. Clean the wheat of any foreign matter
2. Wash it well in a colander.
3. Place it in a saucepan of cold water.
4. Bring to the boil and simmer, adding more water when necessary as the water evaporates.
5. When it is soft, strain it through a colander or a basket and pour plenty of cold water over it until it cools down.
6. It is served with sesame, raisins - blanched almonds and pomegranate seeds when available.

RECIPE 33 OLIVE BREAD

INGREDIENTS
- 5 Cups flour
- 1 envelope yeast.
- Warm water for the dough.
- 2-3 tablespoons chopped onion.
- 2-4 tablespoons olive oil.
- 25 – 30 black olives.
- Chopped fennel or chopped coriander.

METHOD
1. Place the yeast in a bowl with half a cup of hand hot water. (Hot water will kill the yeast; cold water will retard its growth.) Stir it once and let it stand for five minutes. Adding a small teaspoon of sugar will speed up the growth of the yeast.
2. Place the flour in a bowl.
3. Add the dissolved yeast.
4. Add as much water as it is necessary to make a soft and slightly sticky dough.
5. Turn the dough onto a floured surface. Sprinkle both the dough and your hands with flour and knead it thoroughly until it forms a smooth, elastic ball.

6. Cover the dough and let it stand until it doubles in bulk.

7. Turn the risen dough onto the floured board and knead for a few seconds to knock out the air.

8. Divide the dough into two or three pieces

9. Flatten the pieces of dough and divide the olive oil, olives, coriander, chopped mint and onion among the loaves.

10. Shape the dough pieces into balls, flatten them and repeat to spread the ingredients through each loaf.

11. Leave the olive bread to prove and then bake in a hot oven.

RECIPE 34 POURGOURI PILAU

INGREDIENTS

- ☐ Half a cup of noodles.
- ☐ 1 cup pourgouri.
- ☐ 2 Tablespoons cooking oil.
- ☐ 1 Sweet pepper, optional.
- ☐ Chopped tomatoes.
- ☐ Two and a half cups water or broth.
- ☐ Salt and pepper.

METHOD

1. Heat the oil.

2. Add the noodles and stir. Be careful not to over brown the noodles.

3. Remove the seeds from the pepper, cut it in pieces, and add it to the pan then stir.

4. Add the chopped tomatoes and stir for a few minutes.

5. Add the broth or water.

6. When the water boils, add the pourgouri and leave it to cook on a very low flame. If necessary you can add a little more water. Served with yoghurt and salad, this makes a perfect meal.

PROZYMI

In Cyprus, in Greece and I believe in many neighbouring countries, women used homemade yeast, which is known as prozymi, in the baking of bread. One can safely say that a good housewife made the prozymi once a year kept it and looked after it.

On the fourteenth of September, the day of the Cross, the priest blesses the water in the baptismal font, while dipping the cross. After the service, the people kiss the cross and the priest sprinkles the people with the blessed water. He usually uses branches of basil, which every now and then he dips into the blessed water. Many people, mainly women, take some of this water home and they sprinkle it on the heads of the members of the family who did not attend the service.

Some of this water is used in the preparation of prozymi. My mother used to mix one or two spoonfuls of this water with two or three spoonfuls of flour in a bowl. She would keep this bowl covered with a clean cloth in a warm place. After two days she would add another spoonful of flour and mix it with warm water. She would continue to repeat this every two or three days. It would gradually grow as the bacteria in the dough and from the environment started to multiply. When it became the size of an orange, she might take some of this dough and make a couple of pittes for us to eat so that she did not have to deal with a lot of dough. She would continue to add flour and warm water every few days for about forty days. In the meantime, she would use it to bake very few loaves, as she would say, 'the prozymi is still a baby.'

After forty days, the prozymi was quite ready. The night before she would make bread, she would renew the prozymi by adding more flour, mixing with warm water and kneading. She would cover it well, and the following morning it would have doubled in size. She would use it to make the bread and be careful to keep a piece to use the

154

following week when she would bake again. In this way, she managed to keep it until the following year.

Some women take the water from the first rain and they use it for this purpose. In both cases there are plenty of bacteria in the atmosphere. In Cyprus, at least in September, there are a lot of wild yeasts around in the air. . Even today, many women keep prozymi in their freezers. They take it out before they need it, leave it for a while to thaw, and then they mix it by adding flour and warm water ready for next day's baking. Bread made with prozymi keeps better; many people prefer it.

RECIPE 35 HOW TO MAKE BREAD USING PROZYMI

The day before baking your bread, take the prozymi from the freezer and leave it to defrost. I tend to leave it for a day before I renew it to allow it to start breathing. Renew the prozymi by adding one cup of flour, half a cup of warm water and kneading it well until you have a soft dough. This is going to give you a prozymi the size of an orange, which is enough for about 2 kilos of flour. For bigger quantities, make more prozymi

INGREDIENTS
- *Prozymi the size of an orange. You can use two teaspoons dry yeast as well if you want quicker results.*
- *Two kg of flour. I use one to one and a half kg whole meal flour and the rest plain flour. I teaspoon salt.*
- *About three cups warm water with one teblespoon honey.*
- *Three to four tablespoons oil. (Quite often I omit it.)*

155

METHOD

1. *Make the prozymi the night before. If you are going to do more batches of bread, make more prozymi and use only what you need for each bake. If you want to save prozymi save some before you add the yeast.*

2. *Place the flour in a bowl with the salt and any spices you fancy. I use ground cumin that is traditional in the wheat growing areas of Cyprus, which are now occupied.*

3. *Make some space in the bowl and place the prozymi. Add the warm water gradually with the honey and the dissolved yeast if you are using any.*

4. *Work the prozymi very well with your hands and start working in more and more flour until all the flour is used. Continue kneading until you get a soft dough.*

5. *Cover and leave in a warm place until about double in size, (about one to one and half-hours, if you are not using yeast).*

6. *Turn the dough onto a lightly floured work surface and knead with your hands to knock the air out.*

7. *Shape the loaves to fit about three big loaf tins or six small ones.*

8. *Leave to prove and bake in a hot oven at 200°C.*

RECIPE 36 POTATO BREAD

My grandmother often made potato bread. I'm certain that she followed no family recipe; it was her own ingenuity. Perhaps it happened that one day she did not have enough flour, or she had too many potatoes, which had to be used. Some years ago I came across a good recipe for potato bread. I like this recipe because it has an interesting flavour and it rises quickly.

INGREDIENTS

- ❑ 750 g. potatoes.
- ❑ 3 teaspoons salt.
- ❑ ½ cup tepid reserved potato water.
- ❑ 1 tablespoon dried yeast.
- ❑ 2 tablespoons olive oil.
- ❑ 3 –4 cups wholemeal flour.
- ❑ 2 cups ordinary flour.

METHOD

1. Wash, peel and cook the potatoes well in water to which two teaspoons of the salt have been added.
2. Reserve ½ cup of the potato water, drain them, and cool them very well.
3. Stir the yeast into the reserved potato water, which should be warmed if already cool, and leave to rest for about five minutes.
4. Place the potatoes in a bowl and mash them well. Continue beating and add the dissolved yeast and the olive oil.
5. While still beating, add the two kinds of flour and the rest of the salt. In the beginning the dough will be very dry, but as you continue to work the dough, it will become quite soft.
6. Leave to rise until about double in volume.
7. Then take the dough out of the bowl and knead it for a few minutes to knock the air out. Divide the dough in half and shape two loaves. Leave them to prove.
8. Brush the loaves with water and bake in an oven heated to 200°C.
9. To get a crusty bread, spray the oven walls with water, close the door immediately to trap the steam, then put the loaves in.

This is one of my favourite bread recipes. It is not mine, but it is a recipe I have been using for years and have adapted to my needs. This particular one I bake for Green Monday as it contains no fat and no milk and the sultanas give it that extra taste. It keeps moist for several days and it is good with cheese too.

INGREDIENTS

☐ 4 cups whole-wheat flour.
☐ 2 3/4 cups ordinary flour.
☐ 1 teaspoon salt
☐ 4 teaspoons yeast
☐ 1 cup sultanas or raisins
☐ 1 /3 cup honey
☐ 2 ½ cups warm water.

METHOD

1. Put the 2-½ cups warm water in a bowl with the four teaspoon yeast and the 1/3-cup honey, stir, and leave for ten minutes. If the yeast is instant you can use it straight on the flour.
2. Gradually add the flour and the salt. Add the raisins and incorporate them into the dough.
3. Take the dough out of the bowl place it on a board and knead for a few minutes folding and pressing at the same time. At this point you may need to add 2 to 3 tablespoons flour as you knead until the dough does not stick to your fingers. This dough should be a little softer than ordinary bread dough.
4. Place the dough back into the bowl, cover and leave it to rise. It should become double in volume
5. Turn the dough out on a floured work surface and knead with your hands to knock the air out.

6. Divide the dough in two and form two loaves. Place on a baking sheet that has been sprinkled with whole meal flour and leave to prove.
7. Before you put in the oven brush with water and slash some lines on the top. Place in a preheated oven at 215°C for 30 minutes lower the heat to 200°C and bake for another 20 min until when knocked on the bottom it sounds hollow.
8. If you like a crusty loaf throw two tablespoons water at a time three times every three to four minutes during the first ten minutes of baking.

RECIPE 38 MACARONI PASTICHIO

Macaroni Pastichio is a lovely dish. It consists of the pasta, of the sauce bolognaise and the sauce mornay. It is served in buffet dinners, as a whole meal, or as a first course.

INGREDIENTS FOR THE PASTA
❑ 1 packet thick macaroni about 450 grams.
❑ 1-2 cups grated cheese. I use half halloumi and half dry anari.
❑ Water or chicken broth to cook the macaroni.

FOR THE SAUCE BOLOGNAISE
❑ 300 or more grams minced meat. Half pork and half beef.
❑ One finely chopped onion.
❑ Two grated tomatoes or tomato paste.
❑ ½ cup dry red wine, optional.
❑ Finely chopped parsley, fresh or dry mint.
❑ Salt, pepper and cinnamon.

- ❏ *6 tablespoons cooking oil.*
- ❏ *6 good tablespoons flour*
- ❏ *1 litre milk or milk and some chicken broth where the macaroni was cooked.*
- ❏ *Grated cheese*
- ❏ *Two eggs (Optional)*
- ❏ *Salt, if the cheese is not very salty. White pepper, cinnamon and a little nutmeg*

METHOD

1. *Cook the macaroni in salted chicken broth or salted water.*
2. *Transfer the macaroni to a colander saving some of the chicken broth in case you like to use some in the sauce Mornay.*
3. *Add about 2/3 of the cheese and make sure that the macaroni is well covered.*
4. *At this stage, place half the macaroni in a well-greased heat-proof dish.*
5. *Spread the sauce bolognaise over it in the dish and add the rest of the macaroni.*
6. *Cover the macaroni with the sauce Mornay.*
7. *Sprinkle with plenty of grated cheese.*

SAUCE BOLOGNAISE

1. *Place the mincemeat in a thick-bottomed saucepan with a little water to prevent if from sticking and cook for a few minutes. Some people prefer to fry it instead. Add the finely chopped onion.*
2. *If you are going to use wine pour it in now and leave the mince meat to cook longer.*

160

3. *Add the salt, pepper, cinnamon, mint, finely chopped parsley and the grated tomatoes and leave to cook. If necessary add some water.*

SAUCE MORNAY

1. *Pour the oil into a thick-bottomed pan and heat lightly.*

2. *Remove from the heat and add the flour mixing it well.*

3. *Place it back on the cooker and cook the mixture very carefully without browning it.*

4. *Remove from the heat and add about a third of the milk or some of the macaroni water.*

5. *Place it back onto the cooker and stir carefully till boiling.*

6. *Add the remainder of the milk gradually. Bring to the boil and boil for a few minutes*

7. *Cool a little, add the well-beaten eggs and put back onto the cooker for a very little time.*

8. *Take off the cooker and add some of the cheese. Taste and season.*

9. *Pour on top of the macaroni and sprinkle with the remaining cheese. (At this point it can be frozen)*

10. *Before you place it in the oven scatter a few pieces of butter on top. Cook in a moderate oven for about forty-five minutes until well browned.*

One can supplement the minced meat with cooked spinach or with a variety of vegetables.

CHAPTER 22 - PULSES

Pulses are the dried seeds of the legume plant family, which includes all kinds of beans, peas, lentils, chickpeas and numerous others. Many varieties of pulses are grown all over the world, and they are used in many different ways. They are widely used in the Mediterranean, where they were until recently often the main source of protein.

The traditional ways in which the Mediterranean cook combines pulses with vegetables and grains, and sometimes complements with fish, represent what the nutritionists recognise today as the ideal combination for a healthy diet – known as the Mediterranean diet.

Some pulses, such as the haricot bean, need to be soaked overnight. However, they can be quickly prepared by soaking some in water for an hour or so before cooking. Haricot beans, known as 'fasolia,' are widely used in Cyprus. They are served boiled on their own, or with a variety of vegetables like celery, lahana, (Swiss Chard) carrots, courgettes and even fresh beans, accompanied by oil, lemon juice, tomatoes and black olives. In the village they were always boiled with wild vegetables the women collected from the fields.

Leftover fasolia can be made into a plaki for the next day's lunch. Put the fasolia into a saucepan; add some onion, oil (part can be olive oil) tomato juice or grated tomato, a drop of water and simmer. If you are not a vegetarian, you can add some bacon or lountza. It is a beautiful dish, especially on a cold day.

Black-eyed beans (louvia) are another kind of pulse widely used in Cyprus. They are usually boiled with greens and quite often in the winter it is cooked with the yellow squash to make a tasty and colourful dish. To give the louvia a nice white colour, add some lemon juice just before you turn off the heat after cooking. These are served with olive oil and lemon juice. If there is no fish available to complement the dish, open one or two tins of tuna fish which makes a good addition.

Since pulses were a staple food in Cypriot villages every family tried to produce as many kinds as possible or to purchase the necessary amounts to last through the winter. Dried broad beans would be purchased in June, they would be cracked open, aired in the hot sun, and put away for winter use. Even today many housewives purchase the dried broad beans and a grandmother or an old aunt will sit on the floor to crack them open.

As it was important that the beans last all through the winter, different methods were used to kill the embryo so that no insects would develop in the stored beans. Sometimes the beans were put in the hot oven after the bread had been baked, or they were immersed for a few seconds in boiling water and then put out to dry. In this way, the use of pesticides was avoided. Today, the Cypriot housewife has developed modern methods - she puts the beans in the freezer for about forty-eight hours and then she lays them out in the hot sun for a few days.

The merchant has already treated what you can buy in commercial packets. I prefer to buy my pulses from the farmer as soon as they are harvested and preserve them myself. Nutritionists believe that by combining pulses and grains, a protein of a very high value is obtained. An example of this is a dish called 'moutjendra,' which is a delicious combination of green lentils and rice.

INGREDIENTS

- ☐ 1½ cups green lentils, water to cook them.
- ☐ ½ cup celery stalks cut in small pieces.
- ☐ ½ cup carrots in small pieces.
- ☐ Juice of 1 lemon.
- ☐ 3/4 cup rice.
- ☐ For the garnish.
- ☐ 2-4 tablespoons olive oil.
- ☐ 1 onion cut in rings.
- ☐ 1 tomato.
- ☐ 2 slices bread, cubed.
- ☐ 1-2 tablespoons vinegar.

METHOD

1. Boil the lentils until they are tender.
2. Add the vegetables and the lemon juice while the lentils are cooking.
3. When the lentils are tender, add the necessary water, boil, add the washed rice, and cook. While the dish is cooking, prepare the garnish.
4. Heat the oil. Add the onion and brown lightly.
5. Add the bread in cubes, fry.
6. Add the tomato in small pieces and fry.
7. Add the vinegar and simmer for a few minutes.
8. Pour on top of the moutjendra.
9. This dish should have the consistency of a pilau.

RECIPE 40 CHICKPEAS WITH TAHINI - HUMUS DI TAHINA

INGREDIENTS
- About 150 grams chickpeas soaked overnight.
- Juice of 2-3 lemons to taste.
- 2-3 cloves garlic.
- Salt.
- 150 ml tahini.
- Garnish
- 1 tablespoon olive oil.
- 1 teaspoon paprika.
- 1 tablespoon finely chopped parsley. A few black olives.

METHOD
1. Soak the chickpeas overnight.
2. Boil the chickpeas in fresh water until they are soft. The cooking time depends on their age and quality.
3. Drain the chickpeas .
4. Put the chickpeas in the blender; to make blending more successful add some lemon juice or some liquid.
5. Add the remaining ingredients and blend to a creamy paste, adding more liquid if necessary.
6. Adjust the consistency and the seasoning.
7. Pour into a serving dish and dribble a little olive oil mixed with paprika on the surface.
8. Sprinkle with chopped parsley and decorate with black olives.

Chickpeas are an interesting and nutritious legume. When combined with a cereal like pasta, they make a first class protein. Nowadays one can find split peas. The peas are soaked for about eight hours in cold water, drained and placed out to dry. When they are completely dry they are taken to the mill where they are split. In the past they had to be winnowed at home but recently the mills have been equipped with a special fan, which gets rid of the bran.

If whole chickpeas are to be cooked they have to be soaked overnight in warm water and be split by rolling a rolling pin, a bottle or other device over them. Chickpeas are also used in the making of hummus.

INGREDIENTS
- ❏ *1 cup split peas.*
- ❏ *4-6 tablespoons oil or according to taste; half of it should be olive oil.*
- ❏ *Plenty of vegetables chopped up. I find onions, spinach and carrots a must. But you can use any vegetables you have in the refrigerator, like celery, sweet chard, courgette, the outside leaves of the cabbage and the lettuce, some parsley, and if available some mint and basil.*
- ❏ *Two or three tomatoes grated or tomato paste.*
- ❏ *Half a cup of pasta, preferably a small kind, half cooked.*
- ❏ *Salt, pepper and a pinch of sugar.*

METHOD
1. *Cook the chickpeas in water for fifteen minutes or until half cooked.*
2. *Add the oil and the chopped onion.*

3. *Add the grated tomato or the tomato paste dissolved in a little water and cook for a few minutes. Add the pinch of sugar to counteract the acidity of the tomato.*

4. *Add the necessary water.*

5. *Add the chopped vegetables after it starts boiling*

6. *When it comes to the boil add the half cooked pasta to the pan of chickpeas.*

7. *Season and simmer until well cooked.*

CHAPTER 23 - OLIVE OIL, A FOOD OR A MEDICINE

Olive oil is one of the three staples, the others being wheat and

An old oil press - It was pulled by animal or by a person

wine, accompanied by green vegetables they constitute the Mediterranean diet. Olive oil has been called the green medicine. In Cyprus and especially in the villages olive oil was massaged on the neck in case of a sore throat, on the stomach or on the back or anywhere they had an ailment. It did not perhaps cure but it certainly gave some comfort. "He bound up his wounds, pouring in oil and wine." (St Luke Chapter 10 verse 34).

169

It has now been scientifically proved that people with a Mediterranean diet, rich in olive oil, have a lower rate of heart disease than people in the western world. It is believed that it helps prevent bowel cancer, delays aging and lowers total cholesterol.

Unfortunately in Cyprus, I do not know what happens in the other Mediterranean countries, people have now adopted a more affluent diet which together with the lack of enough physical activity and, I believe, the insecurity the Turkish invasion brought, led to many cases of heart problems.

The olive tree, Olea Europaea, has been growing in Greece and Cyprus for more than six thousand years. According to the Greek Mythology the Greeks wanted to change the name of their capital city. Both goddess Athena and god Neptune wanted the city to be named after them. Neptune (or Poseidon as he is otherwise known) offered the trident, or the winged horse, both symbols of war. Athena offered the olive tree a symbol of peace and stability and useful at the same time. Goddess Athena won and the city was named after her.

In the Orthodox Church, olive oil, wheat and wine are taken to church as offerings on many occasions. The olive oil is used as fuel for the lamps which hang in front of the icons. Many Christians take a bottle of olive oil to church when they go for special prayers. The other two staple foods also have religious significance - wheat is taken to church as kolliva for a memorial service or for a festive religious holiday along with bread, and wine is offered for Holy Communion. This triad of the Mediterranean diet has been given a place of honour in the church. On Palm Sunday, women take olive leaves to church; they are left there for forty days to be blessed. These olive leaves are burned in a special pot, the kapnistiri, and at the same time a prayer is said. The kapnistiri is passed around to everybody present who each in turn makes a wish or a prayer. This usually takes place as the sun sets especially on a Saturday afternoon or before a big event.

Fifty or so years ago hand presses were used for the extraction of the oil from the crushed fruit. The olives, after they were picked and washed were taken to the hand press. They were placed in a big stone mill. In the middle of the mill there was a big cylindrical stone called lithari; lithos means stone. The lithari was moved around either by a mule or manpower to crush the fruit. The fruit was stirred to ensure complete crushing. It was then transferred into flat baskets made from palm leaves, or from the leaves of river shrubs. These baskets were placed in the screw type press and manpower was applied to squeeze it down to press the baskets with the crushed fruit and extract the oil.

The first oil, which came out before any pressure was applied, was always collected by my grandmother and used for special occasions specially when the children were sick. This was known as unpressed oil. The oil that came out from the first pressing was classified as cold pressed or virgin oil. In this system pouring boiling water over the crushed fruit in the baskets often speeded up the extraction of oil. When this oil was taken home, it was left for a few days in the containers it was originally collected until all the sediments and the small impurities settled in the bottom. It was then transferred into the final containers. Cold pressed oil is more aromatic and most of the vitamins like vitamin E are not destroyed.

In the Paphos area and in the Karpas Peninsula, the olives, after they were cleaned of the leaves and the other foreign matter, were immersed in hot water and left for about ten or fifteen minutes. They were then taken out and placed in big baskets made of cane for the water to drain. After this, they were placed on old pieces of material made of hemp. I am told that in Paphos they were placed on fig leaves, as they did not have enough rags. They covered them for a couple of days until they became mouldy and then they were taken to the hand press.

In the Karpas Peninsula the olives were immersed in hot water or placed in the wood oven after the bread was taken out, placed on mats to drain completely and the following day were taken to the hand press mill. In both these cases the olive oil, which was extracted, was dark and it is known as black olive oil. I do not think that this method is applied these days. The day they brought the oil from the mill was a day of good eating. They would perhaps make dough, roll it out in pittes or still better they would make bread and dip the warm bread in the fresh oil with some salt. It was delicious.

To make the terms pure, virgin or extra virgin olive oil clear, I quote from the International Olive Oil Council's newsletter. 'The grade of the oil is determined by the oleic acid content of the oil and by standards of flavour, colour and aroma. Pure oils are those oils, which have been refined to remove naturally occurring impurities. Some amount of virgin oil is added to these pure oils to enhance their flavour. Extra virgin oil must not have more than one percent acidity and virgin oil not more than 3.3 percent.' After the olives are pressed and the precious oil is collected, the crude oil cake (zivana) is left behind to be used in many different ways. I remember my grandmother throwing a couple of handfuls of crude olive cake in the burning oven to start a blazing fire. The crude oil cake is a good source of energy. It is made into cakes and burnt in fireplaces and even in power stations.

Crude oil cake has a 50% moisture and between 8% to 12% oil which is mostly olive seed oil. This oil can be extracted with the use of several solvents. The olive seed oil is not only of lower quality but there are valid reasons to think that the solvents used may make the oil carcinogenic. Recently the Institute of Agricultural Research has found a way of fermenting the Crude Oil Cake to produce animal fodder and so supplement the diet of sheep, goats and cows.

In Cyprus many varieties of olive trees are cultivated. The native olive tree, the Cypriot variety, is very old. It gives a high yield of oil, which is known for its characteristic aroma. Another variety, which has been imported from Crete, the Coroneiki, is seen in fields and pavements alike. It grows quickly; its fruit is very small with a high yield. The oil has a beautiful aroma and very low acidity

There are many more varieties which have been imported from Greece like Calamon and Amfissis, good for preserving. Manzolino has been imported from Spain; it is good preserved both as green and as black as it can be harvested in two stages. Other varieties suitable for preservation are the Sevillano, the Cortal and many others.

THE PRESERVATION OF OLIVES

Olives have been a staple food for all the Cypriots especially for the village people. When the children came home from school as the mothers were away on the fields they found bread and olives in a small basket suspended from a hook; if they were lucky there might be some halloumi or dry anari.

When the farmer went to work on the fields to cultivate his land he would take with him a piece of bread with some olives. They always carried the olives in a beautiful pot made of palm leaves called eleopotiro meaning olive cup. These special containers were made in Lacatameia, and they were a work of art.

Every housewife would preserve olives. If she did not have her own fruit she would buy or help other women to pick theirs, who in return would give her some fruit. They preserved mainly the black olives, which lasted a whole year although many of them preserved the greens in different ways. My grandmother, and later my mother, would preserve the black olives in earthenware big pots (pitharia) which had been covered inside with a layer of tar to make them non porous and not to be affected by acids. They would place the blessed olive leaves in the kapnistiri on top of a burning coal, they would then crush a carob and place it on top. When the carob started burning along with the olive leaves the room was filled with a beautiful aroma. The pithari was placed upside down on top of the kapnistiri. In this way the pithari was fumigated and any odd smells disappeared.

These days there are different varieties around; there are many ways of preservation. The basic rules are the same.

1. The olives must be picked by hand so they will not be bruised

2. Those which are going to be preserved green should be picked round October, just when they start to change from bright green to yellowish green.

3. They are washed and crushed lightly. They are known as tsakistes, which means crushed.

4. The next step is to soak the olives in water so as to lose some of their bitterness. The water is changed twice a day. Olives, which are going to be used immediately, are soaked for 5 or 6 days. Olives which are going to be kept for some time are soaked for about 10 to 12 hours. It is recommended that lemon juice be added to the water in the proportion of one lemon to every litre of water. The lemon juice helps the olives keep to their green colour and remain crunchy.

5. The olives are placed in brine. Some people, like one of my cousins who makes excellent olives, makes a strong solution by using one cup of salt to every 6 ½ cups of water. The Agricultural Department recommends one cup of salt to every nine of water. The brine should cover the olives completely. Some olive oil is poured on top. The containers are covered with aluminium foil which is perforated to allow the evolving gases of fermentation to escape. The fermentation lasts for about 40 days; at this stage the containers should be kept in a dark cool place. After this stage the foil is removed, some olive oil is poured on the top of the olives and the containers are closed tightly

Black Olives.

1. The olives should be picked when they are ripe; they should be without blemish.

2. They are soaked for one day.

3. They are placed in baskets to drain and they are left in the sun for two days.

4. They are washed again and placed in the containers; one handful of salt is sprinkled after two or three handfuls of olives are placed .The proportion is about one kg of crystalline salt for every nine or ten kg s of olives.

The containers are well closed. They must be rolled at least twice a week for the first month and once a week later. There are many more ways of preserving olives some much more sophisticated, as there are more varieties. I have described the standard village way.

An earthen cask (pithari) for storage

CHAPTER 24 - THE MAKING OF HALLOUMI CHEESE

Halloumi cheese is the most important type of cheese produced in Cyprus where it originated. Halloumi has been made on the island for many hundreds of years. It is a semi hard type of cheese; traditionally preserved in saline solution, it kept for a long time. In saline solution, halloumi matures, and acquires a new flavour. As it matures, it becomes slightly porous and the fat held in the pores gives it this special aroma. It becomes harder and it grates very well. This is the halloumi people knew and used for years. These days, halloumi is packed in polythene bags and it is frozen. In this way the halloumi remains soft and it does not become saltier. Its colour is white but as it matures it becomes slightly yellow.

Halloumi from cow's milk is yellowish and it becomes more yellow with the passing of time. Traditionally halloumi is produced from sheep and goat's milk. With the increase in the production of cow's milk halloumi started to be made with cow's milk or combined with either sheep or goats milk or both. Halloumi made from cow's milk is inferior in flavour, aroma and appearance.

The yield of halloumi from sheep's milk is higher than the yield from goat's milk and goat's milk is higher than cow's milk. The yield of halloumi depends on the chemical composition of milk and mainly on the content of casein and fat in the milk.

The temperature of the milk when the rennet is added is important. Milk is heated between 32°C-35°C and enough rennet is added to bring about the curdling of the milk in 30 - 45 minutes. In the summer, the temperature should be lower than in winter.

177

The curds are cut up in very small grains, heated slowly up to 38°C - 40°C where they are left for about fifteen minutes and are stirred all the time until the grains acquire the desirable composition. The curd is collected with a ladle and placed in special pieces of material and pressed to get rid of as much of the whey as possible. When the curd is well drained it is cut in pieces and placed in the hot whey after the anari has been collected. (Anari is a softer cheese which is a by-product of halloumi making). The whey is heated gradually to boiling point until the pieces of halloumi come to the surface. They are left for about fifteen to twenty minutes to cook and then taken out and left to cool to about 60°C. About fifteen grams of salt is added to each halloumi and some mint leaves if that is desirable. These are then folded in two and left to cool completely.

When the village women made halloumi they would try and fill at least one big earthenware container, which they left to mature and use during the year. At the same time they would fill a smaller jar to use immediately.

The big container had to be looked after very well. They had to make sure that the pieces of halloumi were kept well in the whey. To achieve this they took a piece of cane scraped it, washed it, cut it in two, crushed it so as to make it more manageable, and then placed it crosswise on top of the halloumi. In this way the halloumi was secured under the whey. They threw some whole peppercorns in the container and then they poured in a little olive oil. A thick piece of material was tied very carefully around the mouth of the container. In this way the halloumi was protected from the cheese flies which would in time turn into little white worms which, although harmless, are repulsive. During the process of fermentation, which lasted 40 days, the halloumi would produce some scum. The village women called this 'the sickness of the halloumi,' and it had to be taken out every five or six days. In 40 days the fermentation was complete, the halloumi was a little harder, saltier but much more aromatic. Very

178

often, when the container was opened after the fermentation was finished, some milk liquid butter would accumulate on the top of the halloumi. The village women would collect this butter very carefully and use it to fry eggs and halloumi. They were delicious.

The cheese factories place the halloumi in jars, which are filled with whey. The jars are well sealed and left in a cool place to reach the desirable fermentation for up to forty days. After this, the jars are placed in refrigerators. Nowadays in cheese factories the halloumi is left in the whey for two or three days and then it is packed in plastic bags hermetically. They are then placed in refrigerators or freezers. The halloumi we eat to day, although very appetising is not quite the same as the mature halloumi we used to eat as children.

ANARI

Anari is a by-product of halloumi and of the other hard cheeses. It is prepared from the whey after the curd is taken away. It is the milk protein, albumen and globulin, which are found in the milk in solution, and they are left behind after the curdling with some of the fat.

THE PREPARATION OF ANARI.

The whey is heated gradually and stirred lightly and, when it reaches the temperature of about 65°C - 70°C, some milk is added for a better yield. The heating is continued until the temperature reaches about 85°C. At this stage, grains of anari start to appear on the surface and we stop stirring but the heating is continued. When the anari starts to take shape and to break at some points, the heat is reduced to very low, and is left to cook for a while. It is then collected with a ladle and it is placed in a special piece of material and pressed to drain. It is cut in pieces of about 10 cm and it is used unsalted or it is slightly salted. The unsalted anari is eaten with sugar or honey and

179

cinnamon or carob syrup. Recently, some cheese factories have begun to market unsalted anari in special plastic containers, which weigh one kg. Anari is served in bowls with the whey and either sugar or honey. Cinnamon and nuts are usually added.

When the village women made halloumi they would send anari with the whey to their relations, their friends or neighbours. Salted anari can be eaten fresh or slightly dry. When quite dry it is very good for grating. Unsalted anari is used in filling pourekia or for making a beautiful dessert with phyllo pastry, anaropitta.

When both the halloumi cheese and the anari were finished the village woman who was preparing the halloumi would share out all the whey left between the vessels that the other village women brought in the morning and left. The whey would be mixed with bran and fed to the pig. If mothers were working in the fields, their children were instructed that when they came home from school they should go pick the vessel with the whey and feed the pig.

RECIPE 42 ANAROPITTA

INGREDIENTS
- ☐ About ½ a kg phyllo pastry. It should be 21 leaves.
- ☐ 2 –3 tablespoons butter melted.
- ☐ 750 grams fresh unsalted anari.
- ☐ Sugar to taste .I use ½ a cup.
- ☐ About 2 teaspoons ground cinnamon.
- ☐ 2 or 3 tablespoons orange blossom water
- ☐ A little milk if necessary.
- ☐ 150 ml fresh cream.

1. Separate the pastry in three, seven leaves in each bundle.
2. Brush each phyllo pastry with the melted butter.
3. Place each bundle in a baking tin. I place each bundle on top of the tin and cut them to the size of the tin. The three baking tins should be of the same size.
4. Place the tins in a preheated warm oven. 150°C until they get a nice golden colour.
5. In the meantime beat the anari with the sugar, the cinnamon, if necessary a little milk, the orange blossom water and the fresh cream if it is to be included. It must become creamy and be easily spread.
6. Place half of the Anari on one of the bundles of Phyllo pastry
7. Place the other bundle on top with the rest of the Anari
8. Finally place the third bundle of pastry on top.
9. Pour a few tablespoons of honey on top and sprinkle some walnuts

RECEPE 43 HALLOUMOPITTA

If you like something savoury with your coffee in midmorning or with your tea in the afternoon, try to make halloumopitta. It is excellent hot but it is quite good cold too.

INGREDIENTS
- ❏ 2/3 cup oil and fat.
- ❏ 4-6 eggs
- ❏ 3 cups flour
- ❏ 4 teaspoons baking powder
- ❏ 2-2 ½ cups grated halloumi, one halloumi grated.
- ❏ 1 cup milk.
- ❏ Fresh or dry mint.

METHOD

1. Sieve the flour with the baking powder
2. Grease and flour a round baking tin with a hole in the middle or preferably one or two loaf tins
3. Break the eggs and separate the yolks from the whites. Beat the whites until quite stiff.
4. In a separate bowl beat the yolks with the oil and the fat.
5. Start adding the flour, the grated halloumi and the milk; then gradually incorporate the mint.
6. Fold in the stiffly beaten egg whites.
7. Bake in a moderate oven of about 175°C for about forty-five minutes.

RECIPE 44 YOGHURT PASTRY

The yoghurt pastry is easy to make it is interesting and any left can be frozen.

INGREDIENTS

☐ 3 cups pastry flour.
☐ ½ cup oil
☐ 1-2 eggs
☐ 2-3 tablespoons yoghurt
☐ 1 teaspoon bicarbonate of soda.
☐ Some tepid water.

METHOD

1. Sieve the flour with the bicarbonate of soda.
2. Place the flour in a bowl.
3. Add the oil, the eggs, the yoghurt dissolved in a little tepid water and mix with your hands and knead until you get a pliable dough. If necessary add a little more water or a little more flour.

This pastry is used in many ways, in spinach pies or cheese pies.

FILLING FOR CHEESE PIES

INGREDIENTS
- One cup grated halloumi
- One piece of fetta cheese
- One piece of unsalted anari or any unsalted cheese.
- One or two eggs
- Some fresh or dry mint.

METHOD
1. Place the grated cheese in a bowl
2. Beat the eggs and add them to the cheese
3. Add the mint and stir well.
4. Roll the dough out on a lightly floured board with a rolling pin or with a pastry machine
5. Place some filling on the dough about one or two inches apart according to the size of the pie you wish
6. Fold the pastry over and seal the edges well.
7. Glaze with egg yolk and bake in a moderate oven until golden brown.

CHAPTER 25 - THE PREPARATION OF TRAHANAS

Trahanas is, along with the halloumi, one of the most valuable foods preserved at home by village women. It is virtually the stuff that makes the national soup of Cyprus. Mothers send their children abroad to study with bags of trahanas. In my village they had a bowl of trahanas soup for breakfast before they went to the fields; unless they were fasting.

For the preparation of trahanas we shall need.

❏ **Milk**. For the preparation of good quality trahanas the milk must be clean and of good quality. Usually sheep's milk or goat's milk is used or a combination of the two. The addition of some goat's milk gives a nice aroma to the trahanas.
❏ **Wheat**. It has to be cleaned of all foreign matter, be washed, dried and taken to the mill where it is ground in thick grains. When it is brought home it is sieved so as to get rid of the flour and then it is winnowed to get rid of the husk.
❏ **Yoghurt culture**
❏ **Salt**

Proportion of ingredients

Usually one kilo of wheat is used for every two litres of milk. I would like to mention here that a relation of mine for every kg of wheat she uses three litres of milk so as to get a milkier result.

185

Preparation.

1. The milk has to be prepared a few days ahead.

2. The milk is strained and heated to about 85°C to 90° C for a short time so that the bacteria are killed.

3. When the milk cools down to about 40° or 45°C the yoghurt culture is added. The village women are able to tell the right temperature for adding the culture by immersing their little finger in the milk and counting up to twelve. If they feel they can just about stand it then it is the right time to add the culture dissolved in some of the milk. If it becomes too hot to stand it then they have to wait and try again. For eight litres of milk about 500grams of yoghurt is enough.

4. The container with the milk is placed in a warm place until it gets the desirable sourness.

5. The milk is heated to boiling point while it is stirred all the time with a wooden spoon. At this stage the salt is added; we taste for salt having always in mind that this will have to be enough for the wheat as well.

6. After the milk boils enough the wheat is added little by little by another person, as we have to keep stirring .At this stage it is safer to have the heat lower. When it thickens and it leaves the sides of the cooking pan we bring it off the heat. It is left to cool until the following morning.

7. The following morning it is kneaded with a little milk, it is shaped in balls and cut in small pieces and put in the sun to dry for a few days.

Recently as many homes have freezers many women have tried to freeze the balls of trahanas in portions to avoid the drying. It is cooked straight as it comes out of the freezer. The advantage is that you can prepare trahanas all the year round. When trahanas is to be dried, in the traditional way, it has to be prepared in the summer to dry well. When trahanas is well dried it is placed in bags made of old material; some pieces of garlic help keep it in good condition.

In the beginning of August the milk they were milking from their goats was not enough to make into halloumi even if they cooperated with the other women in the group, they started to save it and make into trahanas. Their ingenuity was remarkable. They had a good size earthenware pot (kouza), which they placed, in the coolest part of their house. Around this pot they put gravel and sand, sometimes they even threw some barley, which germinated and kept the container even cooler. They made sure that the pot was scrupulously clean. After they milked the goat they left the milk to cool down completely, they strained it and poured it in the jug. They put a good handful of salt. They threw plenty of water round the jug to keep it cool. In the evening they added more milk. Every time they stirred the milk with either a wooden spoon or with their hand having washed it carefully. The stirring of the milk by hand would help one feel the consistency of the milk. After five or six days they added more salt. This went on for at least fifteen days sometimes as much as twenty two days. The jug was kept very cool with the sprinkling of water and the growing barley. The milk was tasted and if it had the right acidity and the right consistency it was ready to be used. Quite often we were given a little to eat before they started to make the trahanas in the usual way. In those days you could not walk into a shop and buy yoghurt, at least not in the village.

RECIPE 45 HOW TO COOK SOUP TRACHANAS

Trahanas is a very interesting soup with a lovely flavour and a beautiful aroma. At the same time it is very nutritious as it is made of sour milk and ground wheat. One can buy trahanas from a village woman who makes it at home for her family and to supplement her income, from a supermarket or a cheese factory.

INGREDIENTS *(For four people).*
☐ *240 grams trahanas*
☐ *Water or chicken broth.*
☐ *A good piece of halloumi cheese.*

METHOD
1. *Place the trahanas in a saucepan add some cold water and leave for a few hours to soak.*
2. *Place the saucepan on medium heat and stir until it starts to boil. Lower the heat and leave it to cook for about half an hour.*
3. *Add the halloumi in small pieces and let it boil for a few minutes on low heat.*

If you like a finer soup put it in the blender. In my village they would poach eggs in the soup and dish out an egg for each person. In this way it becomes a very substantial meal.

CHAPTER 26 - FIGS

Figs are an excellent fruit, characteristic of the Mediterranean. Many homes in Paphos or on the lower mountains of the island will have one or two fig trees in their yards. Figs are picked early in the morning; Cypriots love them for breakfast. If they had plenty, some were dried for winter use.

In Cyprus, there were three native varieties: the small green fig, the purple fig known as vasanato (aubergine coloured), and the big green one which used to grow abundantly in the Morphou area and ripened in the late summer. Now there are many more varieties. Some of them start ripening in the early summer, and some until late in the autumn.

Dried figs are high in calcium and phosphorus, elements that are necessary for bone building and body maintenance. They have extremely low sodium content. Three kilos of fresh figs make one kilo of dried figs. One day I had a telephone call from a man who had come back from his holiday to find his fig tree full of figs, and asked if I could tell him how to dry them. I said it would be better for him to be shown how to do it by one of the old ladies in the village since they know best, but I gave him a recipe for fig jam.

In the village of Pyrgos, the small green fig variety grows in abundance. People dried them, sold them locally or exported them. When you had the chance to visit Pyrgos, it was a good opportunity to buy some; dried figs were always sold by weight, in packets or threaded on strings. This was a cottage industry in which all the village women were involved.

To dry figs successfully, an almost airtight room was built outside the houses where the figs were put on special trays. Then sulphur was burnt in the room. To seal the room, the door was plastered with mud. The burning sulphur produced sulphur dioxide, which is both a bleaching and a sterilising agent. This not only killed any insects that were present; it bleached the figs as well, making them white and more presentable. The following day, the figs were taken out of the room and put out in the sun to dry.

Tourism and over development have spoiled almost all the cottage industries, as the village women quite rightly find better paid jobs in the factories and the hotels. Fortunately, there are still a few old village women who insist on keeping some of these beautiful customs alive. In the village of Lyssos the women used to dry the big vasanata, known as 'maxiles'. They were known all over Cyprus and much sought after. The village women would pick the figs, choosing the small green ones, which were easier to dry. They tried to pick them with the stem on, then lay them out in the sun to dry for several days. When all the figs are dried, they are washed in hot water, or dipped for one minute in water which has been boiled with some fennel flowers. The figs are then drained well, and laid on clean cloths to dry completely. They are then sprinkled with flour and stored for the winter. Dried figs can be eaten on their own, combined with nuts, or used in cakes, puddings and fruit salads.

Figs can be served with thin slices of tender ham as a first course. In Cyprus, some varieties of figs are often made into glyco it is delicious.

RECIPE 46 FRESH FIG JAM

Figs are deficient both in acid and in pectin, so quite a lot of lemon juice is needed. They are combined with cooking apples, which are very rich in pectin.

INGREDIENTS

- ❏ 1 kg fresh figs,
- ❏ ½ kg cooking apples.
- ❏ Juice of 6 – 8 lemons.
- ❏ Grated rind of two lemons.
- ❏ 1 kg sugar.

METHOD

1. Wash the figs and peel them.
2. Peel, core and slice the apples. Mix with the figs, lemon juice and rind in a pan.
3. Simmer until the fruit is tender, stirring often.
4. Stir in the sugar over a low heat until dissolved.
5. Boil hard until the jam is set, about 15 minutes.
6. Pour into sterilised jars and cover.
7. If a spiced flavour is liked, put a small piece of cinnamon stick, a piece of bruised root ginger and two whole cloves in a piece of muslin and suspend in the pan while the jam is cooking. Remove these before bottling.

RECIPE 47 FRESH FIG CHUTNEY

INGREDIENTS

- ❏ 1 kg green figs.
- ❏ ½ kg onions.
- ❏ 100 grams crystallised ginger.
- ❏ ½ litre vinegar.
- ❏ 225 grams brown sugar.
- ❏ 2 teaspoons salt.
- ❏ ½ teaspoon pepper.

METHOD

1. *Wash the figs and cut them with the onions in small pieces.*
2. *Heat the vinegar, sugar, salt and pepper until the sugar is dissolved.*
3. *Add the figs, onions, ginger and bring to the boil.*
4. *Simmer until the mixture is thick.*
5. *Pour into jars and cover.*

CHAPTER 27 - THE QUINCE - CYDONIA OBLONCA

The Quince tree has been cultivated in Cyprus since ancient times; it belongs to the same family as apples and pears, though it has never acquired as much importance. It is found on the hills and in the mountain villages, usually it is grown in the yards of village houses or in the orchards with other fruit trees; but there are no large quince plantations.

Today, the quince is a forgotten fruit tree that deserves to be remembered and relished. It is an interesting fruit, with a yellowish flesh, rich in flavour, but it is not eaten raw, as the fruit is hard and full of tannins. Interestingly, the longer it is cooked the pinker the flesh becomes.

In Cyprus quinces have been used for years in the making of glyco, the fruit preserved in syrup; it was one of the traditional glykos to be offered to guests with a glass of fresh water. They are still used for the making of quince paste, kithonopasto, and quince jelly. Since quince is rich in pectin, it contains little acid, and therefore it makes a beautiful jam and an excellent jelly if some lemon juice is added.

RECIPE 48 QUINCE GLYCO

INGREDIENTS
- ❑ 1 kg quinces.
- ❑ 1 kg sugar.
- ❑ The juice of several lemons.

METHOD

1. *Wash and peel the quinces throwing them in cold water acidified with lemon juice.*
2. *Take each fruit and cut four or six pieces according to the size of the fruit and throw the pieces back in the acidified water.*
3. *Throw a few at a time in boiling water for very few minutes.*
4. *Cool them immediately to stop them from cooking.*
5. *Place them in cold water acidified with plenty of lemon juice for a couple of hours.*
6. *Take them out, drain them well and place them on a piece of cloth to dry Place the fruit in a good saucepan with the sugar and some lemon juice*
7. *Leave overnight and boil until it is well set.*
8. *When cold serve in sterilized jars.*

RECIPE 49 QUINCE GLYCO TRIFTO (GRATED)

INGREDIENTS

❑ *1 kg quinces*
❑ *Sugar, one cup sugar for every cup grated quince.*
❑ *The juice of two or three lemons.*

METHOD

1. *Wash and peel the quinces.*
2. *Throw in cold water acidified with lemon juice.*
3. *Grate on the thick part of the grater.*
4. *Measure the grated quince with a cup and use equal amount of sugar.*
5. *Place the grated quince, the sugar and the lemon juice in a saucepan and boil until set.*

This is the glyco that used to be served at weddings on the Sunday after the couple came from church many, many years ago.

The peels can be made into a jelly.

194

RECIPE 50 QUINCE JAM

INGREDIENTS
❑ 1 kg quinces prepared fruit.
❑ 1½ kilos sugar.
❑ 1 – 2 cups water in which to cook the fruit.
❑ Juice of 2 – 3 lemons.

METHOD
1. Peel, core and slice or grate the quinces, and put them in a saucepan with the water to cook.
2. Cook slowly until the fruit is tender. If the water is too much, reduce the volume by boiling the quinces with the lid off.
3. Add the sugar and lemon juice and stir until the sugar is dissolved.
4. Boil rapidly until setting point is reached.
5. Pour into sterilized jars and cover

RECIPE 51 QUINCE JELLY

INGREDIENTS
❑ 2 kg quinces.
❑ 3 littres water.
❑ Juice of 2 – 4 lemons.
❑ Sugar 450 grams for each ½ littre of juice

METHOD
1. Wash the quinces, but do not peel them. Cut them up.
2. Simmer in a covered saucepan with the water until tender. (Approx. 1 hour)
3. Strain through a jelly bag or through muslin. Boil the juice
4. Add 450 grams sugar for each ½ littre of juice and stir until dissolved.

5. Boil rapidly until setting point is reached.
6. Pour into sterilised jars.

If you can find some mosfilo fruit (It is a wild fruit found in Cyprus) combine it with the quinces, it will make a better jelly.

RECIPE 52 BAKED QUINCES

INGREDIENTS
- *6 quinces.*
- *Some butter.*
- *8 – 10 tablespoons sugar or to taste.*
- *Whipped cream or strained yoghurt.*
- *1 tablespoon rosewater if available.*

METHOD
1. *Pre-heat the oven to 200°C.*
2. *Wash the quinces and cut them in half.*
3. *Core and de-seed them.*
4. *Put each quince cut side up on a piece of foil.*
5. *Put a little butter on each and 1 – 2 tablespoons sugar, as the quinces are very sharp.*
6. *Wrap them in foil and bake for an hour until tender.*
7. *Serve hot or cold with cream or yoghurt and add a little rose water.*

On many of the Greek islands, quinces are cooked with pork.

RECIPE 53 HIRINO ME KITHONIA (PORK WITH QUINCE)

INGREDIENTS
- ❑ 2 tablespoons olive oil.
- ❑ 1 kg boned cubed pork
- ❑ 1 onion finely chopped.
- ❑ 1 teaspoon ground cumin.
- ❑ 1 teaspoon cinnamon.
- ❑ 1 teaspoon pepper.
- ❑ 1 tablespoon sugar optional
- ❑ ½ a cup brandy.
- ❑ 1 kg quinces peeled, cored and sliced.
- ❑ 4 tablespoons chopped parsley.
- ❑ 3-4 tablespoons pomegranate seeds when available.

METHOD
1. Heat the olive oil.
2. Add the meat and brown it.
3. Add the chopped onion and stir.
4. Sprinkle the sugar and stir.
5. Sprinkle the cumin, the cinnamon and the pepper.
6. Add the brandy and let it evaporate.
7. Add about one cup of water and boil the meat until almost done. Add more if necessary.
8. Add the peeled, cored and sliced quinces and cook for another half an hour-or until they are tender.
9. Towards the end add the pomegranate seeds.
10. Taste and season.
11. Serve and garnish with plenty of chopped parsley.

In North Africa, quinces are cooked with lamb. This recipe is said to have originated in ancient Persia.

RECIPE 54 ARNI ME KITHONIA (LAMB WITH QUINCE)

INGREDIENTS
- ❑ I large onion, coarsely chopped.
- ❑ 2 –3 tablespoons cooking oil.
- ❑ 1 kg. lamb.
- ❑ Salt and pepper.
- ❑ ½ teaspoon powdered ginger.
- ❑ 1 teaspoon cinnamon.
- ❑ 2 large tomatoes.
- ❑ 1 kg. quince.

For the method, follow the pork recipe.

RECIPE 55 QUINCE PASTE

INGREDIENTS
- ❑ Quinces.
- ❑ Sugar.
- ❑ Water.

METHOD
1. Wash the quinces. Do not peel or core them.
2. Cut them into small pieces.
3. Cover with water and simmer until the fruit is very soft.
4. Sieve or put the fruit in a blender.
5. Weigh the fruit. Allow 1 kilo sugar to 1 kilo of pulp.
6. Mix the pulp and sugar together and stir until all the sugar is dissolved.
7. Boil gently for 45 minutes to 1 hour, stirring all the time to prevent burning. It is safer to cover your hands when you are stirring the preserve.

8. *The quince paste is ready when a spoon drawn across the bottom of the pan will leave a clean line.*

9. *Pour into trays; leave for a few days, cut into pieces and store. Some people dust the fruit with icing sugar, but I prefer not to as I think it spoils the lovely flavour of the fruit.*

CHAPTER 28 - THE MOSFILO TREE

(CRATAEGUS AZAROLUS)

The mosfilo tree is a deciduous and quite often thorny tree. On the plains it can be found on the edge of almost every field. The farmers in my area, protected these trees as they were very useful. They provided shade when they needed to sit down to have their meal. They could tie their goats to the trees as very often when they went to the field they took their goats along. But above all the mosfilo tree provided shade for us, the children, when we were looking after the watermelon fields. We would also hang on one of the branches, our little basket we brought in the morning from home with the precious egg, our bread, the few olives and possibly the halloumi or the anari. A wooden bed was placed under the tree for the father as he used to sleep there at night to protect the watermelons. There we would place our few possessions, and we would build the fire where we would cook our egg with the vegetables we picked from the field. During the long days we used to play a very interesting game with the still unripe mosfilo. We would make six or eight holes on the ground, always under the shade of the mosfilo tree. We would place the same number of the fruit in each hole. Although I do not remember the rest, I recall that the one who finished having all the fruit was the winner.

These trees are found on the plains and on the hills and they grow naturally anywhere the stone happens to fall. The fruit is round, fleshy with stony pits, edible when ripe with an interesting taste. The most common mosfila are fleshy and yellow, although a different variety of red, ovoid mosfila are common in mountainous areas. The mosfilo has been used for years by the villagers. It contains the vitamins A,B,C and many minerals. It is supposed to cure many health problems. It regulates blood pressure, lowers blood cholesterol and has many other health benefits according to the villagers, who use natural products to cure every disease.

The mouflons of Cyprus love the mosfilo fruit very much. When the fruit is ripe they knock the trunk of the tree with their horns, the fruit falls. The rest of the mouflons hear the noise and they run to enjoy the spoils.

This fruit has been used for years by the village women, for the preparation of jelly. My mother used to tell me that when the mosfila were ready, about the middle of October, she, with her aunt Preza, would get one of the donkeys, usually the most cooperative, from the stables, get it ready, place a big saddle bag on it and go in search of the best mosfila. They used to cross the river and go to an area called Lakanes. There they would find the biggest fruit. Perhaps these trees were of a different species. They would fill the saddlebag and come back happy as they had enough not only for themselves but also for their friends and neighbours. If the trees were very tall, and usually they were, they would shake the trees, the fruit would come down and they would pick it, as they had spread some old rugs on the ground.

At this time of the year there were very few other fruit trees around, not only in the villages but everywhere in Cyprus. People had to rely on what they had in their yards or in the fields.

They made jelly out of them, but we children loved to eat them plain. I do not think a recipe exists. People use their instincts, even today. Pick the fruit, clean it, take off the little stem and throw out the rotten ones, wash them well, place them in a big pan, cover them with water and boil until the mosfila are quite soft and some of the water has evaporated. Although there are no rules I estimate that you should be left with a little more than half of the original water. At this stage I add some lemon juice as it helps the pectin to be released more easily.

The liquid is strained through muslin so that a brighter jelly is obtained, it is then measured .It is placed in the pan and then on the cooker and when it starts boiling the sugar is added. For each cup of juice one cup of sugar is added. Just before it is quite finished add some more lemon juice, test for setting and bring off the cooker. It has to be served soon after, as, if you are successful, it starts setting very quickly.

The cooked mosfila are good to eat as well. As I said earlier people use their instinct. Some people get a second brewing, which is weaker, but others, like one of my cousins, once the fruit is placed on the cooker, does not add any more water. I have tried this method. The jelly it makes is very well set but there is much less of it.

The mosfilo tree is a hard bearing tree. For that reason it is used as a subject for grafting pear, quince or polemidhia. Some people started planting it in their gardens..

CHAPTER 29 - WHAT IF?

What if I wake up one morning to be told that I can go home? Just like that, without any formalities, without any previous warning. What shall I feel like? I just do not know. Shall I start thinking about the house, the furniture, the trees, the machinery, my mother's treasures, the boreholes with the cool water or the village in general or what is most important the people? Some of these people have died, some have done well but others are not so happy or so successful.

How is my house going to be? I am certain there is nothing left, no good old furniture. I would so much like to see some of this, like the beautiful walnut piece in the front room, the old carved chests but above all the antique plates and ornaments on the shelf round the walls of the dichoro. But what about my mother's treasures? Her weaving was unique - it cannot be replaced. She bred the silkworms, she made the thread out of the cocoons, and she spun the flax, she made the linen thread, she often dyed her cottons to get the colours she wanted. She made really beautiful pieces, not one or two but hundreds. What she could not make herself she found specialists in Lapithos who made them for her. This was her idea for her daughter's dowry. None of these things can be replaced.

If I knew that these things were taken but loved and appreciated and if they were still a part of the Cypriot culture and heritage, I think I could forgive. Unfortunately they are probably lost for ever, or destroyed, or thrown away, or sold to someone. What about the photographs on the wall of the small front room, the room where guests would be received? The photograph of my grandfather, the priest, the portrait of my parents and parents in law, of my uncle the teacher with his beautiful sisters. I had a photograph, the only one I had as a very young girl, taken with my youngest aunt. I used to like it very much. That is gone too.

What about the orchards? I shall certainly like to visit the orchards in the different parts of the village. Will the trees be green, still alive? Have they been properly looked after, pruned, nourished and watered? Do they still produce fruit? Are the boreholes in good working order? Is there still enough water in the well or has it been exhausted with unwise use? So many questions, so many doubts.

What about the people? Our next-door neighbours, Kyria Morfini had seven children. The three older ones, a girl and two boys were like my sister and brothers. We grew up together and we shared many things. Kyria Morfini, her husband Karazinos, her daughter, and one of the sons died and were buried away from their village. They will not be there but their memory will always be with me. Kyriacos who lived opposite our house, died from a heart attack. There was such a struggle, so much agony to make a living for the family. Our other neighbour Philios, the strange young man with the nice wife, will not be there to play the violin all the times of the day and night. These are memories that make our life richer. They may be painful at times but they certainly gave meaning to our life.

I am sure the camels, which used to live on the field near our house will not be there. I do not even know if Loizos Kamilaris got them out or left them behind. He is dead, I shall probably never find out. This reminds me of Styllou Pantela the first woman to buy cows in the village. She was very successful, she made good money. She fed the cows and left the village planning to come back. She never did.

I understand that all the icons in the church have been stolen and part of the church destroyed. If I go, if we go, we have to work together, all of us to start rebuilding the place. Material things can be dealt with. What about the people, especially the young people, how much do they feel they belong to the village, how committed are they? Before the invasion I knew everybody in the village and everybody knew me and had some special respect for me for various reasons: I was the first girl to leave the village and go to town to a good Secondary School; my father and later my husband helped the village in many ways. The village population must have changed a lot. So many boys and girls married people from other parts of Cyprus and many from other countries. Many young people have built their lives quite successfully in other parts of the island or indeed like my own children in other parts of the world. It is certain that life in the village will be different more difficult, it will need much adjustment. But if and when it happens that we return, those who will have survived, will surely make the effort.

CHAPTER 30 - A SAD VISIT

On the 22nd of April 2003, Denktash opened the frontiers so that the Turks would visit the free areas of Cyprus and the Greeks would visit the occupied area. It was a clever move and so was the timing. The 22nd was the Wednesday before the Greek Easter, and with Good Friday and Easter Monday as public holidays, the response of the Greeks was beyond expectations. The Greeks went either in their cars or they hired a car once they entered the occupied area of Nicosia. Most of them were refugees who wished to see their homes and villages; some went as far as the cape peninsula to pay homage to the church of Apostolos Andreas. Almost everybody visited Kyrenia. The check point was at the Ledra Palace; the people queued for hours. The government of Cyprus provided buses for the Turks to take them to all the towns of the free area of Cyprus.

On the 10th of May a check point for cars was opened at Ayios Dhometios. Matters became easier for both Greeks and Turks.

On the 2nd of June it was to be the big day for us. It was a Monday; we tried to avoid the weekend for obvious reasons.

We set off from Paphos before 7 am. We were at the check point in Ayios Dhometios just after 9 am. It is a very emotional experience. Both sides are very well organised, the people on duty very polite, the environment very clean and fresh with shrubs planted along the road and in the middle of the wide road to make the entry and exit points. The formalities are over very quickly; my husband showed our passports, his driving licence, he paid eight pounds for the insurance of the car and we set off. I cannot describe my feelings. I tried not to look at Nicos so as not to make my pain bigger.

The whole view is impressive. The roads are spotless with shrubs planted on either side. In the background there are many blocks of flats. I cannot believe that so many people got together in this part of Nicosia. Many years before the invasion, part of this place had been bought by the Bank of Cyprus; it was divided in plots and sold to Cypriots, mostly Greeks. It was known as Kermia.

The road to Morphou and to our village is paved on the old railway line. The fields on the two sides are planted with shrubs and young pine trees. It is obvious that they put a lot of work to plan the public places so as to impress the visitor. One becomes certain of this when one visits places which are not on frequent public show. The turning to the village is marked. They changed the name to Akcay. If it was not for the sign we would not have found it. All the way to the village it was raining. This made our visit more difficult. For years I had walked all the roads of the village at all times of the day and night. I had difficulty to recognise which part of the village we were. They brought down most of the old houses which had been built with mud bricks. They did it in an untidy way, leaving parts of the walls standing. The pleasant surprise for me was the rain water that ran through the middle of the village. It reminded me of my childhood years. This rain water ran every winter and sometimes we had a problem to cross the road and go to the opposite side to my grandmother's house. This rain water had later stopped to run through the village as the farmers used to collect it for farming before it reached the village. Unfortunately, I was so moved that I could not enjoy it or come out of the car and paddle in the rain water as I used to do as a child.

At last through untidy and dirty roads we came to the house. A house which lost its pride and dignity, an old house without a character, without any atmosphere. There are none of the characteristics which gave the house the aura of its grandeur. Now it was an old house, untidy, full of pieces of furniture scattered all over the house to accommodate the needs of an old couple from the village of Potamia and their teenage grand children.

210

Gone is the Victorian bed dressed in the hand woven silks. The cupboard made of solid walnut wood is transferred to a corner in another room. I noticed that it was full of stains, or was it scratches. I could not see very well as my eyes were clouded with tears. The decorative piece of furniture which used to adorn the front room of the house is transferred in a corner in the little room adjoining the dichoro. It goes without saying that all the old plates and the merreches which decorated the shelves of the big room are gone along with the big chest and the three bundles of the silk woven materials. They must have been stolen the very first days of the invasion. Gone are the hand carved chests, the antique sofa and everything left behind. The dichoro is divided in two rooms to make bedroom space for all the grandchildren of the couple.

I could not stay longer in the room, I was suffocating. I went out into the iliacos where we used to enjoy our breakfast and dinner and where the children spent many happy hours playing. The floor is in a bad shape but the most worrying is the condition of one of the pillars; part of the stone at one point is half ruined. At the far end they installed a sink for washing up. The huge yard was full of many useless objects and cages of chicken. There were some sheep, a dog and a lot of untidiness. The three ovens were hidden behind a lot of straw. We could not proceed to the stables or the mantra as the junk in the yard made our way through almost impossible.

I am not sure that the roof of the iliacos will take another heavy winter without collapsing. The house had known many beautiful days during my father's days and during our life. As my father was the mayor of the village until his death everybody who came for official work would have his meals with us and quite often would have a bed too. There were the different religious celebrations in church and the blessing of the house by the priest afterwards. A big meal would follow with everybody invited to share it with the priest, the hymn singers and all of us. On Green Monday and Easter Monday we had family friends from Nicosia for the appropriate lunch; a visit to the orange orchards would follow with everybody picking fruit to take with them. Today, the house is in a very bad shape; it is very old, built by the grandfather of my father. If it is not somehow restored it will not be liveable. Under other circumstances it would have been a listed house. It was heart breaking to see it in this condition but we still have the memories of happier times to keep us company.

We got into the car, we had a dry mouth and wet eyes. We proceeded to visit some of the citrus orchards. The first one we visited was a piece of about 35 donums planted with all kinds of citrus. Lemons, all kinds of mandarins, jaffas, valencia's, washington navels, sweet lemons and seville oranges. We could not believe our eyes. We drove in the field as Nicos had built a road with a small round about so as the lorries, which came to get the fruit would turn easily. We saw only cows. In this field there was a borehole with an engine which worked with electricity. Even that disappeared. We went to visit the other orchards, the situation is the same. We saw many shepherds with hundreds of sheep It is obvious that our village has changed its character; from a prosperous agricultural village to a livestock rearing village.

Nicos put a lot of work into these gardens. The children, I and my mother were always there for support. For my son it was a way of life. By doing some work or by supervising the work in the garden he could secure loans from Nicos to buy what he wanted. When the invasion happened he still owed money for the purchase of a cine camera. He was devastated as we all were.

Whatever happened, we still have the memories of a rich life; living on the land in a friendly community, sharing the same problems with people; bringing up our children near the land. We had a lot, we lost a lot, but we gained a lot by living the life the land offers. The land gives you strength. We are richer for that.

INDEX

214